First published in the United States of America in 2011 by
Quarry Books, a member of
Quayside Publishing Group
100 Cummings Center
Suite 406-L
Beverly, Massachusetts 01915-6101
Telephone: (978) 282-9590
Fax: (978) 283-2742
www.quarrybooks.com
Visit www.Craftside.Typepad.com for a behind-the-scenes peek at our crafty world!

10 9 8 7 6 5 4 3 2 1

ISBN-13: 978-1-59253-722-8

Digital edition published in 2011
eISBN-13: 978-1-61058-140-0

Library of Congress Cataloging-in-Publication Data available

Cover Design: bradhamdesign.com
Book Layout: *tabula rasa* graphic design, www.trgraphicdesign.com
Series Design: John Hall Design Group, www.johnhalldesign.com
All photography by Joshua Curry Photography, unless otherwise indicated.

BEVERLY MASSACHUSETTS

Jewelry Lab

QUARRY BOOKS

52 Experiments, Investigations, and Explorations in Metal

Melissa Manley

Contents

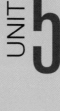

*Lab 22: Recycling Tin
(see page 68)*

Lab 39: Flame Patina on Copper (see page 106)

Introduction

Photo by Robert Diamante

Brooch with squirrel jaw and cloves
by Melissa Manley

*"You have not found your place
until all your faculties are roused
and your whole nature consents
and approves of the work you
are doing."*

—Orison Swett Marden, writer

I WROTE THIS BOOK FOR YOU. I teach people of all walks of life, retired folks, college students, teenagers, hobbyists; but my favorite students are total beginners, those to whom metal has called. They are interested but still fresh like young children, ripe for information about the new and foreign world of jewelry making. It's delightful and exhilarating to spark and share their joy of discovery, to empower them to create with metal.

But I am only one person, and so many of you out there are hungry for more. Believe me, there is an abundance of jewelry-making and metalworking advice and information to share! So I wrote this book. I wanted a format that would allow a little dabbling each week, a chance for you to nibble off small, manageable bites of the huge, delectable metals pie. Without you leaving the comfort of your own home, you and I can easily connect and share the jewelry-making experience.

By completing the 52 labs in this book, you will have finished a beginners' course in metals and jewelry. This format is intended to present the information in a fun and exciting way that reflects my own excitement about experimenting with metal and jewelry. It is by no means an all-encompassing metals encyclopedia, but rather a springboard for a long relationship with jewelry making, one that gets you addicted to playing with metal (the key words being *relationship* and *play*). There's no greater reward for me than hearing about a former student who now drives down the road thinking about ways to connect jewelry parts or dreams about metalworking. I hope that through this book, you too catch this bug and join me on the jewelry journey.

Getting Started

What You Need to Know

This book covers mostly nonferrous metals, or metals without iron in them. The methods discussed apply to silver, copper, brass, bronze, and nickel. Any words in **bold** text appear in the glossary at the back of the book.

We measure sheet metal thickness in gauges. Using a round **Brown & Sharpe (B&S) gauge**, you can measure the metal's thickness by sliding it into the slots around the edge until it fits snugly. Jewelers most often use 24-gauge, 22-gauge, and 20-gauge thicknesses.

Pieces of sheet metal and a round B&S sheet gauge

Sawing

To make jewelry from metal, you must first cut and shape the material into usable pieces with a jeweler's saw. Unlike a hardware store hacksaw, the jeweler's version has wing screws at each end to clamp in a saw blade. The blades come in sizes from #10/0, which has the smallest teeth, on up to #6, #5, #4, and so on. (The higher the number, the smaller and closer together the teeth are.) Jewelers typically tend toward #3/0 or #2/0 blades for the most common metal thicknesses. As you become comfortable sawing, you'll develop your own preferences.

Here's the step-by-step on sawing metal:

1. Load the blade into the saw by clamping it with the wing screw at the tip opposite the handle. To make sure the blade's teeth point downward, hold the blade over a white piece of paper or stroke it against your sleeve (it will pull on the cloth if the teeth face down).
2. Brace the end of the saw against a table edge and push toward the table with the handle as you tighten the blade into the bottom wing clamp. When you let go, the blade should ping when you pluck it, meaning it's under enough tension. This tiny little piece of steel chewing through your metal will use tension as its ally.

Tools to saw through metal

The size and placement of the teeth change depending on the thickness of the metal you want to cut.

Use a V-slotted bench pin like this for easier sawing.

The distance between the saw's body and its blade determines how far into a piece of metal you can cut.

3. Secure a V-slotted **bench pin** in place. This is a wooden tool that you must use while sawing to support your metal and to allow for free movement of the blade. It becomes the action zone for most of your metals processes. Your metal *must* have support underneath each side of the blade for the saw to work properly. Do not saw metal hanging off the edge of a table with no bench pin.

4. To pierce out a design from the middle, drill a hole in the metal you plan to cut. Tighten the top end of the saw blade in place, leaving the bottom loose. Thread the loose bottom (still partially in the saw) through the hole. Slide the metal all the way up on the saw blade to the top. Brace the saw against a table at a downward angle so the dangling piece of metal is out of your way as you hold the saw handle, push forward, and tighten the bottom end of the saw blade in the saw. You may have to stand up to do this until you get the hang of it. Now you're ready to saw.

5. Relax. This step is important. Remove the concept of *sawing* from your mind and instead envision yourself *stroking* the metal with the saw. The less you force the blade, the better.

6. Hold the metal as you transfer it to the bench pin so it doesn't snap your blade. Place it flat on the bench pin with your blade in the V-shaped opening.

7. Begin sawing. Gently move the blade straight up and down—don't tweak it sideways, that will kink and eventually snap the blade. Two or three soft upward strokes will help start a trough to begin sawing.

The throat depth of a saw—the distance between the saw's body and the blade—determines how far you can cut into a large sheet of metal. If your only option is a shallow saw, back it out and turn the sheet around to saw the opposite side.

Be prepared to break many blades—order at least a couple dozen!—as you learn to use subtle pressure. Remember, the more you force the saw, the harder it gets, and vice versa. If you force it, you pay a price.

Saw Blade Specifications

Use this chart to determine the proper drill size and blade you are using.

Blade size	Blade thickness	Blade depth	Teeth per inch	Recommended for: (B&S gauge)	Drill size for piercing
8/0	.0063"	.0126"	89.0	up to 26	80
7/0	.0067"	.0130"	84.0	24–26	80
6/0	.0070"	.0140"	76.0	24	79
5/0	.0080"	.0157"	71.0	22–24	78
4/0	.0086"	.0175"	66.0	22	77
3/0	.0095"	.0190"	61.0	22	76
2/0	.0103"	.0204"	56.0	20–22	75
1/0	.0110"	.0220"	53.5	18–22	73
1	.0120"	.0240"	51.0	18–20	71
2	.0134"	.0276"	43.0	16–18	70
3	.0140"	.0290"	40.5	16–18	68
4	.0150"	.0307"	38.0	16–18	67
5	.0158"	.0331"	35.5	16	65
6	.0173"	.0370"	33.0	14	58
7	.0189"	.0400"	30.5	12	57
8	.0197"	.0440"	28.0	12	55

Commercial waxes, beeswax, or oils can lubricate saw blades and facilitate sawing.

Tips

Apply a very gentle downward stroke, to allow the teeth of the saw to chew through the metal. Also, try these sawing tips:

- Angle the blade slightly forward when sawing a long, straight line.

- Move the blade up and down, perpendicular to the floor, for easier turning. Sawing metal is not like sawing wood; it's done up and down, not horizontally.

- Signs that you're pressing too hard when you're sawing? White knuckles or a grimace like a tiki face. These signify that you're probably using too much pressure. If you still have trouble, try a finer saw blade (signified by a higher number).

- Keep your saw moving up and down when backing out of a cut. If you can't back out or don't want to, loosen the screw and pull out the loose blade.

- Lubricate saw blades with beeswax, oil, or commercial burr lubricants.

Drilling

First things first: When drilling, wear safety glasses. To start drilling, use a **center punch** (a pointed metal toll for making a divot or dimple in metal) to strike a poppy seed–size dent or divot in the metal. This allows the drill to stay exactly where you want it and not travel around leaving a gouged track. After the initial hole, move to a slightly larger drill bit; spin it in the hole's back side to rake off the sharp burr (or edges) caused by the drilling. It will even give you a counter-sunk hole (a hole that is beveled and has angled walls) if you are aggressive with it, essential for accurate flush rivets.

A center punch makes divots in metal using a small chasing hammer.

A drill bit in a pin vise can remove a burr caused by the bit.

Annealing

Annealing means softening with heat. It's done when you need more malleable metal. Just as muscles can tighten up after an aggressive workout, metal can stiffen and harden after excessive hammering or working. This is called **work hardening**. When metal is too hard, it can crack or break. To alleviate this, we heat the metal with a torch. This allows the space between the molecules to expand. The metal remains butter-soft until you work it in some way again.

The annealing process can happen over and over again on the same metal sheet. In fact, you might anneal a piece dozens of times while hammering and shaping it. To anneal a piece of metal:

1. Heat up the piece until it comes to a dull glow, not a bright orange.
2. **Quench** it in water. Wait a few seconds before quenching silver so as not to shock it, especially Argentium sterling. Do not quench brass, nickel, or bronze after annealing, but rather allow them to cool off on their own. They should remain pliable.

After annealing, your metal should, in most cases, look black with sooty **firescale** caused by metal oxidation. If not, you may not have heated it to the appropriate temperature. Clean off firescale by sanding it or using a mild acid called **pickle**.

Metal being annealed

Pickling

The solution for this metal-cleaning process is called *pickle* because it's much like what's used to pickle vegetables, combining an acid and a salt. (Traditional jewelers' pickle is most often **sodium bisulfate**, though there are other options.) Look for the brands **Sparex** or **Rio Grande**. You'll most likely purchase it as a dry granular acid and then mix it according to package directions with water. It works best warm, so jewelers often use crock pots to keep up the temperature. A few other tips: Don't allow it to boil, ventilate the area in which you're working, and keep baking soda on hand to neutralize spills.

Wearing gloves, an apron, and goggles, and shielding yourself from splatter with something like the crock-pot lid (the pickle may bleach fabric and does irritate skin if it comes into direct contact), carefully lower the metal piece into the solution with copper tongs. The pickle cleans away the firescale by eating oxidized copper molecules off of the metal. This can take anywhere from five to thirty minutes. Over time the pickle becomes a super-saturated solution, like a copper-filled sponge, turning blue as it fills up. At a certain point, it quits cleaning. When this happens, remove any metal from it, take it to a sink or place it in a plastic tub to catch spills, and slowly sprinkle in baking soda. It will fizz and foam. You can dilute it with a trickle of water and continue adding baking soda until it stops foaming. Contact your local waste-management agency to find out the best method of disposing of these hazardous materials. Once saturated, pickles are loaded with copper molecules and can wreak havoc on local water treatment plants. Do not pour it down the drain!

A solution of 1 tablespoon (18 g) of salt for every 1 cup (235 ml) of household vinegar may also work as a pickle. *Always* rinse your work in clean water as soon as you take it out of the pickle so you don't dribble acid on your floor or clothes.

Working with Torches

If you plan to work your way through this whole book, you'll have to use a torch in your jewelry-making adventures. Start with a simple gas/air torch, which you can find at your local welding-supply store. As you grow and add more skills to your repertoire, this torch will accommodate you well. It is simple to use, requires

Tip

To remove the slightly pink copper plating from brass and bronze caused by pickling, use a vinegar-and-hydrogen-peroxide mixture. Or try soaking it in equal parts pickle and hydrogen peroxide, sometimes called *nickel pickle*, *super pickle*, or *50/50*.

A Smith air/acetylene torch, tank system, and tips

Charcoal blocks and solderite boards make good soldering surfaces.

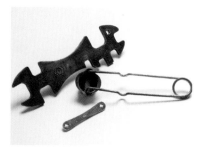

Other options: plumber's propane bottle torch, a crème brulée torch, or an oxy/gas mini torch

Tank keys and a striker

no oxygen, and usually goes for about 200 dollars, with the tank. (At some point, you may decide it's time for a gas/oxygen system such as a mini torch, but for the labs in this book, an acetylene/air or propane/air torch is fine.)

You need a heatproof surface to work on. Tile board or cement board, sometimes called HardiBacker, can protect a surface from heat, but you also want some sort of commercial soldering pad for direct heat. You need a small charcoal block for some solder operations and for fusing pure metals such as silver. Soldering accessories such as **third hands** (bases that add an extra level of stability) are essential as well. See Resources, page 142, for suppliers. Universities with metals programs sometimes offer metal and tools in their bookstores, as do jewelry schools with supply stores open to the public.

Tanks

The most important part of your gas tank is the little square pin sticking out of the top. (Some tanks have a small knob covering this pin and do not use a key.) Either way, never let this fragile piece break off. It allows the chamber to open and close, letting gas into the hose and regulator. If it breaks, it turns your tank instantly into a missile. Though it won't explode, the tank will shoot backwards with enormous force, crashing through anything in its way. Protect the pin by chaining the tank upright against a wall. Here are a few other tank pointers to follow:

- Never leave a tank key in place after you use it to turn on the tank. Remove it.
- Use only a small key to turn on the tank, not a tank wrench. The latter could put too much force on the pin.
- Allow your tank to settle for an hour before lighting because some gases, especially acetylene, are mixed with fillers.
- Never use machine oil, three-in-one oil, or oil of any kind for that matter on or near your tank. Oil is a petroleum product and is flammable when mixed with some gases. It will also melt the protective seals inside the torch.
- Test for leaks by going over joints with soapy water. The leaks will blow bubbles, allowing you to detect and correct them.
- Keep the air/acetylene tank pressure under 8 psi.

While it may seem scary at first, learning as much as you can about your tank and torch empowers you to move past your reservations.

Filing

Jewelry files, used to shape metal, remove material, and smooth edges, come in many shapes and sizes. There are large files that cover a broad area and allow you the most evenness, and large specialty hand files in finer cuts such as a Swiss #2 and #4, or German #3 and #5 are precision-made and have finer teeth. Half-round files work both flat and curved surfaces, and small files such as needle files get into small areas easily.

Think of these files as hundreds of saw blades clamped together. Their teeth cut in only one direction: away from you. As you file, always brace the metal against a table, desk, bench pin, or filing block. Never air file; like air guitar, it's pointless and makes you look ignorant. Learn to file with or along an edge rather than across it. The latter method chatters or catches the file, preventing it from moving smoothly, and may even cause stair steps or scallops along your metal's edge. Finally, employ a small vise, clamping work holders, or a **wooden ring clamp** to keep whatever you're filing in place.

Sanding

To sand metal, you'll use wet/dry (sometimes called waterproof) sandpaper. This is more durable than regular sandpaper and can be moistened, which cuts down on dust and lubricates as you sand. It typically ranges in grit coarseness from 220 to 1,500, getting finer the higher the number you go. Cut the paper into small pieces you can fold and use or into strips you can insert into a split **mandrel** (a tool used for finishing metal). You can glue it to paint stirrers or Popsicle sticks, or you also can tape it down to a table.

When sanding broad surfaces, start with a coarser grit, such as 220 or 320, and sand in one direction only. When appropriate, move to a finer grit and sand in the opposite direction. Change sanding direction each time you move to a finer grit. It allows you to sand out scratches from the previous grit.

The regulator on your tank regulates the amount of pressure on the gas and shows gas level.

Jewelry files shape metal, remove material, and smooth edges. A wooden ring clamp helps hold work in place.

Wet/dry sandpaper varies in coarseness, from 220 on the coarse end to 1,500 on the fine end. Put them on Popsicle sticks or tongue depressors for easy use.

A steel split mandrel for finishing with a strip of sand paper inserted in a flexible shaft machine

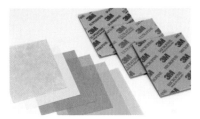

In this book, we use 3M sanding pads in superfine, microfine, and ultrafine to hand-finish pieces.

Finishing and Polishing

A book's worth of material could cover the myriad ways to finish jewelry. Tools such as a Dremel, a flexible shaft machine (a rotary motor with a long shaft that accepts attachments), or a buffing machine work well. Experiment with various attachments to get the finish you want. For the labs in this book, sanding pads in superfine, microfine, and ultrafine will work well as hand-finishing tools. Your hands remain the best tool. Machines merely supplement when our hands can't do the trick.

Some of the more common finishing and polishing tools include:

- Extra fine steel wool or a 3M pad. This generates a more hand-made finish.
- Buffing wheels and compounds. Use these to polish up to a mirror finish.
- Spectrum finishing papers. These allow you to finish and polish metal by hand without any special tools.
- Yellow silver polishing cloth. Use this for a final buff, but beware that you could be merely polishing up scratches. It can actually make scratches show up more clearly. There is nothing worse than a whitewashed rotten fence, so if you choose a high-polish finish, fine-sand thoroughly.
- Blackening **patinas**. These accentuate texture. **Liver-of-sulfur** patina is an easy one to use and the most innocuous because it doesn't contain any acid. Dip the metal into the freshly mixed patina, and then rinse, finishing as desired.
- Jeweler's brass brush. Unlike hardware store brushes, this brush has very fine, soft bristles and can produce a lovely sheen. Lubricate it with a little soap and water, and brush your work after dipping it into liver-of -sulfur. (If you need to remove more patina to show off texture, buff the jewelry with a 3M green scrub pad or very fine steel wool, and then brass brush again.)

Tools

In addition to knowing proper techniques for jewelry making, you also need some tools in your arsenal. Here are a few to start with. If you don't see something listed here, check the glossary at the back of the book for more information.

Hand Punches

Hand punches look like giant hole punchers, and they have much the same effect, just on sheet metal rather than paper. Read the instructions for your particular punch, and insert the male and female dies correctly. If you don't, the punch will simply make a big dimple in the metal.

These tools cost approximately forty dollars (£25), are portable, and make it easy to create large holes without having to drill.

Hand punches cut clean holes through metal.

Dapping Block

A **dapping block** is a steel cube with multiple cavities and often comes with a set of matching, round-ball end punches in a wooden stand. The punches force dome shapes into a round circle of metal. Use the appropriate corresponding punch, usually a bit smaller than each depression or you risk leaving a circular ding forever on your dapping punch. Then, every time you use it, it will emboss your circle with the damaged mark. Annealing your metal before dapping will allow it to dome more easily.

Using the dapping block and a punch on a piece of round metal can create a dome shape.

Disc Cutter

A **disc cutter** is a special tool that allows you to chop perfectly round circles into sheet metal. Though they appear heavy and strong, the punches are a delicate, often expensive tool that you must treat kindly. In particular, protect its outer sharp edge, because it's what does the cutting. It spirals down as you strike the opposite end with a heavy brass hammer, shearing off the metal in a circular motion.

Here's how it works: Place a sheet of metal through the tool's slit, and then choose a punch corresponding to the size circle you want. Hold onto the punch, and then hit it with the hammer. (Holding it prevents it from bouncing up and down in place in the shaft of the cutter, which can cause it to get stuck.) Do your punching on a heavy wood stump, on an anvil, on the floor, or on a piece of leather. The leather protects the punch when it breaks through, and the floor gives you resistance, which helps the punch do its job. The tool isn't a necessity— you *can* saw out circles by hand—but it sure makes life as a metalsmith easier.

A disc cutter allows you to make perfectly round circles out of metal without having to saw.

Making an Impact

WHAT DOES IT MEAN to make an *impression* or an *impact*? These phrases conjure all kinds of pictures. Contrary to popular thought, metal is extremely malleable. From the moment we figured out that we could shape metal, our destiny changed. We suddenly could make hard implements and tools in all sorts of shapes, and we no longer depended on chipped stone blades that were so tedious to make.

Metal is much like clay, but moves slower and sometimes requires force greater than your fingers. Keep this image in your mind throughout this unit. Metal can be impressed with texture using varying amounts of force. In fact, it may surprise you how little can create a distinct mark.

A sterling textured cuff made by Nick Mowers

Texturing with Hammers

In this lab, make as many marks as possible using a wide variety of hammers. Pay attention to how the metal moves as you hammer. If the metal bows up, flip it over and flatten it with a soft rawhide or rubber mallet. How does the shape of the hammer's face affect the mark it leaves?

- copper washers
- wet/dry sandpaper
- shears
- files
- center punch
- hammers (French riveting hammer, chasing hammer, any other hammers you have)
- drill or hole punch
- metal block
- rubber mallet, optional

"A thousand words will not leave so deep an impression as one deed."

—Henrik Ibsen, playwright

Earrings made of hammer-textured washers

Instructions

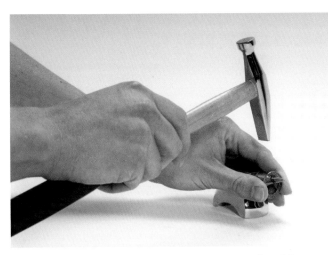

Edge-thickening a washer with a hammer on a small anvil horn

1. File and sand down edges on your copper washers until smooth.
2. Hammer a center punch (a pointed metal punch) lightly with a small chasing hammer to make a tiny mark or dimple called a divot. Drill or punch a hole to attach **findings**, the jewelry components that make them wearable, such as clasps or hooks.
3. Take the riveting hammer and over a metal block, repeatedly strike the washer with the back end or cross **peen** end of the hammer.
4. Try the chasing hammer next. With the face, hammer blows that partially overlap each other.
5. Use only the ball peen end of the chasing hammer.
6. Make overlapping marks with any of the hammers you have before you.

Experiment

On a hard wooden surface, stand a piece of metal on its edge. While holding it, hammer repeated blows using the back end of the riveting hammer. Watch as it spreads the metal's edge. This is called *upsetting the edge* or *edge thickening*.

Examples of various hammer textures on washers

Tip

The position of your hand on the handle affects the blow. For more control, grip the lower part of the handle and allow the weight of the hammer's head to do the work.

LAB 2 Found Texture

Materials & Tools

Look around you for heavy steel in your environment or objects you find when taking a walk: manhole covers, sides of large hammers, washers—you can use any weathered piece of steel to emboss texture onto your metal.

- metal
- objects to hammer against (old manhole covers, sides of carpenter's hammers, concrete, beat up pieces of metal)
- patina
- shears (or disc cutter)
- sanding pads
- files
- hammer
- pliers, optional

Left to right: *Grinder marks on an old train piston embossed onto metal; copper hammered on a manhole cover; clock gears embossed onto metal; copper hammered on a machine part with etched lettering*

Instructions

1. Cut small pieces of metal that you'll later texture.

2. Smooth down all edges by sanding and filing.

3. Search out pieces of steel against which to hammer, such as manhole covers, weathered surfaces of metal, concrete, and so on.

4. Lay the metal face down on your chosen surface. Hammer on the reverse side of where you want the texture, the side that's now facing up. Lift up the metal now and again to see what's happening. If necessary, use pliers to hold the metal as you hammer so you don't hammer your fingers.

5. Using a disc cutter, shears, or a saw, cut out shapes from your textured sheet.

6. Buff the surface, if needed, and add patina. A liver-of-sulfur patina will enhance the texture.

Tip

When you construct jewelry, create your found texture first, and then cut it to shape. Also, use a hammer with a smooth, slightly curved face. And don't strike too hard. It will squish the metal just like clay and may bend in a direction that you don't want it to.

Experiment

With this lab, experimenting is the name of the game. Keep your eyes peeled for any objects that can withstand hammering. Even visit your local metal recycling facility; it often has leftover steel pieces that make fantastic texturing blocks and tools.

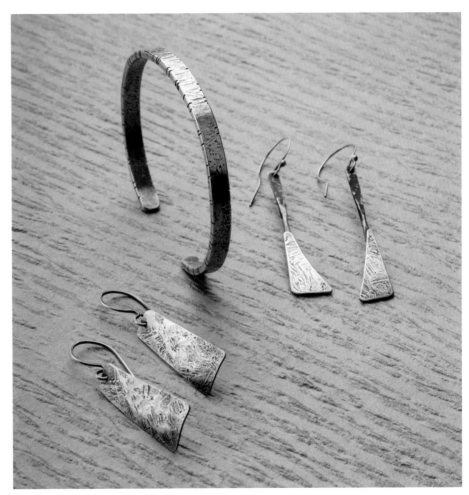

Earrings and bracelet that employ found texture

LAB 3 Homemade Texture Hammers

Materials & Tools

- metal
- nails (or other tools to rough up a hammer's surface)
- 2 hammers or old ball peens
- vise
- center punch, optional

"A man of genius makes no mistakes; his errors are volitional and are the portals of discovery."

—James Joyce, writer

You can modify hammers using punches, files, grinders, or high-speed burrs. You can then use these hammers to make embossed or raised texture on metal.

A bronze bracelet made of convex round pieces textured with a modified hammer

Instructions

1. Anchor a hammer face up in a vise.
2. Using a nail or center punch, hammer dots into the hammer's face.
3. Prepare pieces of metal to hammer.
4. Try out your new texture hammer.

Experiment

Rather than a nail, try using a big, rough file to rough up the hammer's face. If you have an angle grinder, you might also try that to gouge the hammer's face. Or try using an old hammer that you found at a yard sale or in your garage. Carpenters' hammers have been roughed up in their use and create wonderful texture.

Tip

Wear goggles and gloves to protect your hands and face during this process, especially if you use a grinder. Also, double check that you've safely and securely anchored the bottom hammer before hitting it.

Try different techniques to create unique textures on your hammer's face.

Simple Forged Cuff

- 6 inches (15.2 cm) thick copper or silver wire (4- or 8-gauge)
- hammers (riveting, raising, and forging hammers)
- metal block or anvil
- pliers, optional
- soft mallet, optional
- bracelet mandrel, optional

"If you would hit the mark, you must aim a little above it."

—Henry Wadsworth Longfellow, poet

To add interest, variety, and sturdiness to your jewelry, try varying thicknesses and widths in a heavy wire by spreading out strategic areas. Practice on thick copper ground wire, which is available at hardware stores. Be sure to strip off the plastic if it's coated.

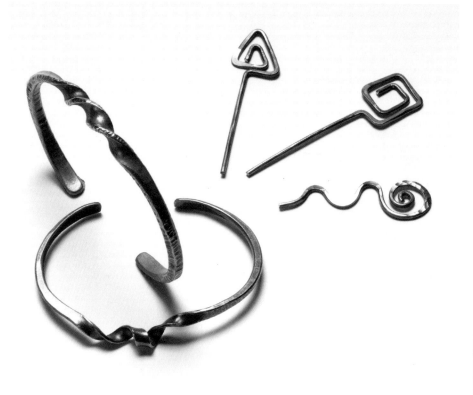

Examples of forging used to create interest

Instructions

Left: *Start with a hairpin shape, forged only at the curve with forged paddles at tips.*

Center: *Bend the legs of the wire out into a split.*

Right: *Notice the side view of the curve's beginning.*

1. Hammer the ends of thick wire such as 4- or 8-gauge to spread it out. It should look like a canoe paddle.

2. Make a tight U shape, like a hairpin, in the middle of the wire. Hammer at the curve of this pin only. This will cause the wave in the metal.

3. Spread apart the legs of the U-shaped pin, one toward you and one away from you, in scissor-kick fashion.

4. Flatten completely.

5. Form into a cuff bracelet. If it's stiff, anneal it to shape it. You should be able to curve the cuff with your hands. If not, use pliers wrapped with tape or leather, or plastic-jawed pliers. Or hammer with a soft mallet around a rolling pin or commercial bracelet mandrel, if you have one.

Experiment

Try exaggerating a curve in wire using only the hammer and no pliers. Also, experiment with different hammers: a smooth-faced hammer for less texture, or a round-faced for small hammer marks. How do the faces create different results? Finally, using the back end of a riveting hammer or a cross peen, leave texture on high spots or across the wide area you already forged out. Try making more than one wave on the same bracelet.

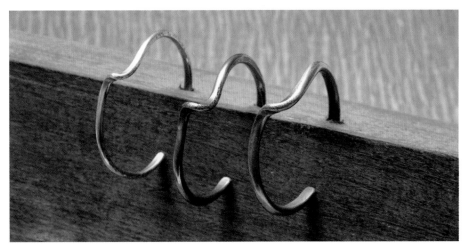

Forged cuffs in copper and silver

Tips

- If the wire becomes too stiff, it will crack. Anneal it with the torch until the metal gently glows, and then cool it. It should blacken as you move the torch away. If it doesn't, heat it more. (You will need to pickle off the black firescale.) Don't worry about rushing; the metal stays annealed until you hammer or bend it again.

- Practice so you can control the hammer blows to get the result you want.

- Too much force will warp your design.

Patterns with Letter Stamps

- metal
- wet/dry sandpaper
- steel letter stamps
- liver-of-sulfur patina
- buffing pad or extra-fine steel wool
- commercial ear wires or chain
- saw
- snips, optional
- disc cutter, optional
- file
- steel bench block
- center punch
- chasing hammer
- drill
- pin vise with drill bit
- rawhide mallet, optional

Believe it or not, ordinary letter stamps make great, out-of-the-ordinary patterns. Think in terms of symmetry and asymmetry, and use repetition to your advantage. Or stamp with punches over wood or leather from the backside of the metal to produce interesting bumps. Try not to think of the stamps as letters but as designs, and turn them sideways and upside down.

Examples of necklaces made with letter stamps

Instructions

1. Shape two pieces of metal using a saw, or cut the metal with snips, or punch out discs with a disc cutter.
2. File and sand the edges.
3. Mark a divot using a center punch to drill a small hole in each metal shape.
4. Stamp in patterns with the letter stamps and your chasing hammer.
5. Drill an ear wire hole, and using the bigger drill bit in the pin vise, clean off the remaining burr.
6. Repeat until you have your desired patterns.
7. Patina the metal with liver-of-sulfur and buff off the high spots.
8. Attach to ear wires or chain for a necklace.

Tip

When you use a letter stamp, hold it down with one hand and strike it once with your hammer. Don't lift up the stamp yet! Instead, while holding it in place, tilt or angle the stamp toward you and strike again. This should get a good impression, hopefully without creating a double impression.

Experiment

Flip over your metal shape and hammer using the center punch from the backside. Do this on a block of wood to create little raised bumps on the front. This (or simply flattening it with a rawhide mallet) will also counteract the cupping effect that occurs when you stamp too much on one side.

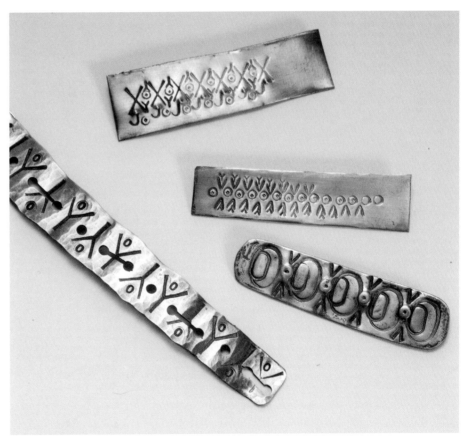

Get creative using these stamps by turning them sideways and upside down to make interesting designs. Examples by Gabriel Vohryzek Lombardi

Leaving an Impression

THIS UNIT TEACHES one method of making an impression on metal that doesn't require force: etching. It's a fun way to apply surface design to metal.

In the etching process, acids, often called *etchants* or *mordants*, eat away at exposed areas of metal. Different acids work on different metals. For the labs in this book, you need ferric chloride etchant and powdered citric acid. (See Resources for places to purchase them.) Though it's actually an iron salt, ferric chloride solution works like an acid on certain metals. It is easy to use and is often employed to etch circuit boards. Muriatic acid, a form of hydrochloric acid, also works, but it is much stronger, can burn skin, and creates hydrogen gas as it etches. The fume causes chemical burning of the nose and lung tissue, requiring ventilation in your work area. This book focuses on ferric chloride, which is much safer. If you wish to try others, there's plenty of information about etching mordants out there. Always practice safe usage, read directions, and be conscious of your local hazardous-waste removal procedures.

Ferric chloride is a yellow liquid that etches brass, bronze, copper, steel, and nickel. It works best when combined with powdered (anhydrous) citric acid; the formula's developer, Friedhard Kiekeben, called the combination Edinburgh Etch.

UNIT 2

You can find this dry citric acid where fabric dye is sold. For copper, combine 1 ounce (30 g) of powdered citric acid dissolved in warm water to 16 ounces (475 ml) of ferric chloride solution (or a one-pint [475 ml] bottle). Prepare separate Edinburgh Etch baths for each type of metal being etched, etching brass separately from copper, etc. Mixing them will contaminate your bath. (You need to use a different mordant to etch silver, so the projects in this unit use brass, bronze, or copper, only.) Never etch zinc or aluminum in this bath as these can have dangerous chemical reactions.

For etching, you need a shallow glass dish or plastic container such as a baking dish with a lid or a plastic shoebox. You can use the lid as a tray to carry dripping acid-covered metal to a sink. There are also inexpensive commercial etching bubbling tanks you can purchase from circuit board etching suppliers. You also need a resist, any material that blocks the acid, thereby protecting the metal. To help you remember, a resist *resists* acid. Some examples include commercial varnishes, transfer papers, spray paint, clear packing tape, and paint pens or permanent markers. There are also commercial resists called asphaltum and "hard grounds." StazOn solvent ink for rubber stamps makes an excellent resist.

Once you adhere the resist, submerge the exposed metal into the bath. Here's a good way to do it: lay packing tape sticky-side up, and then place your metal face up onto it and adhere. Using the long pieces of tape as handles, flip over the metal and suspend it face down in the acid, sticking just a little of the tape to the rim of your bowl or plastic container. The newer the acid, the faster it eats or "bites" into the metal. The more it's been used, the longer it takes, as it fills like a sponge with metal molecules.

Once the metal etches to your liking, remove it from the acid and bathe it with ammonia. Rinse it thoroughly. As an added precaution, neutralize and clean further by scrubbing the surface with 1 tablespoon (14 g) or so of baking soda. Again, rinse thoroughly. Now your metal is ready to be made into whatever you choose!

A super-saturated solution no longer bites and you must properly dispose of it. Do not pour this solution down any drain! It will eat your pipes and ruin the city water treatment facility. Instead, use a funnel to pour it back into its container and take it to hazardous waste. In a small studio, you may get a year or more out of a single pint bottle.

Bronze bangle etched with DNA patterns by Gail Marcus

Ammonia and baking soda are used to neutralize ferric chloride.

Examples of sheets ready to etch and already etched

Etching with a Paint Pen

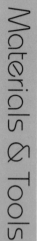

In this lab, you learn to use hobby store paint pens as an etching resist. The ferric chloride eats away metal where you haven't put paint and the copper is exposed. Once it's cleaned and the paint pen resist is removed, the lines will be raised above the metal's surface.

- plastic or glass container
- ferric chloride
- ammonia
- baking soda
- metal, 20-gauge or thicker
- paint pen
- packing tape
- gloves
- eye protection
- newspaper
- paint remover or turpentine
- solder, optional
- pickle, optional
- sanding pads, optional
- patina, optional
- snips
- dish scrub
- saw, optional

Metal etched with a paint pen

Instructions

Using tape as a handle, lower the metal into and remove it from your etching solution easily.

1. Mix your etching solution.
2. Cut out a square of metal with snips.
3. Clean the metal using a green 3M dish scrub with soap and/or swab on denatured alcohol, or anything that may degrease and leave the metal fingerprint-free.
4. Draw, write, or doodle with a paint pen on the metal's surface.
5. Lay out approximately 1 foot (30.5 cm) of packing tape sticky-side up. Lay the metal face up in the middle of the tape and stick it down.
6. Fold over the extra tape at either end, and using the new handle you created, flip over the tape and metal. Lower this into the ferric chloride until acid covers the whole face of the metal decorated with paint pen.

Tip

Inserting a **scribe**, pin, or fine pencil point into the etched area can help you determine whether it's finished.

Experiment

Play with paint pens that have tips of different diameters. To create variety of depth and line, before you etch or after you've partially done so, scratch back through dried paint pen and etch some more.

7. Wait 20 minutes to 1 hour depending on the newness of the acid. Check periodically.
8. Put on gloves and goggles again, and then use the container lid as a tray. Lift out the metal and tape and take it on the lid to a sink. Pour about 1 tablespoon (15 ml) of ammonia on the metal's surface, and wash it under running water.
9. Take off the tape and scrub the metal with baking soda. Rinse it clean. Now you can saw, solder, pickle, or work the metal in any other way you'd like, or buff it with sanding pads and patina, if desired.

Another example of etching using a paint-pen resist. Paint pen resist has been removed on the left revealing the writing.

Blue Magic! Etching with PNP

- plastic or glass container
- ferric chloride
- ammonia
- baking soda
- black-and-white artwork
- PNP transfer printing paper
- paint pen
- newspaper
- gloves
- safety glasses
- packing tape
- shears
- tweezers
- metal spoon
- agate burnisher
- household iron, optional

Press-N-Peel or PNP is blue transfer paper used in the past for etching circuit boards. In this lab, you learn how to laser print or photocopy onto PNP to make unique designs in your jewelry. Black-and-white artwork like line art, drawings, or letters work best with this transfer paper. The toner will burn onto the PNP paper and can then be ironed onto metal.

A copper dirigible etched using PNP paper

Instructions

PNP paper peels off when cool, leaving toner adhered to the metal's surface.

1. Mix your etching solution.

2. Photocopy or laser print (do not use an inkjet printer) your line art onto the soft, matte-finish side of the PNP paper. You will probably need to run it through the bypass tray of a copy machine, the flip-down tray on the machine's side. This can be selected on the machine, as if you were making a transparency.

3. Cut and clean a small piece of copper to etch. Be sure to degrease and scrub it with soap.

4. Lay your metal onto an electric burner of a stove or another heat-resistant surface.

5. Lay your PNP, artwork-side down, onto the metal and hold it in place with a pointed tool or tweezers. (Once it is hot, wear gloves to protect your hands.) As it gets hot on the stove burner,

Tip

Remember to reverse any text either on the copy machine using "mirror" or in a computer photo program. If you don't, your words will etch backwards.

Experiment

Try changing between positive and negative images to etch different parts of an image. You may also try different methods of adhering the transfer to find what works best for you. Fill a page with multiple types of images to copy since you'll have a whole sheet of PNP. This way, you'll find what type of images work best.

burnish the image down using something like an agate burnisher or the back of a spoon. It may take quite a bit of heat and possibly pressure. Or lay your artwork on your metal, cover it with newsprint or thin fabric, and iron to adhere it.

6. Gently lift up one corner of the PNP to see whether it's sticking.

7. Allow it to cool in place. Do not remove the PNP until the whole piece has cooled (this usually takes only a few minutes).

8. Lift off the PNP. The acid will etch wherever there's exposed copper. Touch up with a paint pen any areas you don't want etched.

9. Tape off the back of the metal and etch.

Burnishing a PNP transfer onto metal on a hotplate

Spray Paint as a Resist

- glass or plastic container
- ferric chloride
- ammonia
- baking soda
- metal
- spray paint
- packing tape
- goggles
- gloves
- patina, optional
- sharp tool, such as a scribe or needle
- saw, optional
- sanding pads, optional

"We are what we repeatedly do. Excellence, then, is not an act, but a habit."

—Aristotle,
Greek philosopher

Spray paint can work as a cheap, easy resist. Cover a whole piece of metal with it, and then draw through it with any sharp tool. The acid will eat in the lines where you've exposed the copper.

A bracelet made using spray paint as a resist

Instructions

1. Mix your etching solution.

2. Clean a piece of metal.

3. Spray the metal evenly with spray paint and allow it to thoroughly dry.

4. With a sharp tool, draw, write, or doodle through the paint, just like scratch art from grade school.

5. Lay out approximately 1 foot (30.5 cm) of packing tape, sticky-side up. Lay the metal face up in the middle of the tape and stick it down.

6. Grab the handles created by the leftover tape, and wearing gloves and goggles, lower the metal and tape into the ferric chloride so acid covers the whole face of the metal.

7. Wait 20 minutes to 1 hour, depending on the newness of the acid. Check periodically. Inserting a scribe, pin, or fine pencil point into the etched area can determine whether it's finished.

8. Put on gloves and goggles, and then use the container lid as a tray. Lift out the metal and tape and take it on the lid to a sink. Pour ammonia on the metal's surface, and wash it under running water.

9. Take off the tape and scrub the metal with baking soda. Rinse it clean. Now you can saw, solder, pickle, or work the metal in any other way you'd like, or buff it with sanding pads and patina, if desired.

Experiment

Test different types of scribing tools, different types of marks, and a variety of line thicknesses. Thicker lines allow more contact and should etch better. If you are good at cutting, try making stencils to spray through.

With a sharp tool, draw, write, or doodle through the paint to create your design.

Tip

To remove the spray paint, sometimes just a green dish scrub pad will do. If that's not enough, paint thinner on a cotton swab should do the trick.

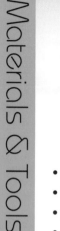

- steel
- ferric chloride
- glass or plastic container
- resist material of your choice
- packing tape
- newpaper
- gloves
- safety glasses
- hammer

"A discovery is said to be an accident meeting a prepared mind."

—Albert Szent-Györgi, scientist and Nobel Prize winner

In Lab 2, we learned to hammer against hard, textured objects to emboss texture onto your metal. In this lab, we make our own designs etched onto steel to make thick plates, against which we can then hammer for texture. Check your local hardware store for pieces of steel, or ask a local metal shop to cut a piece of mild steel for you to make into your texture plate.

Ring and jewelry embossed with texture from a steel plate

Instructions

Hammer against designs etched onto steel to create texture

1. Mix your etching solution.
2. Choose a design and an etching method from those we covered in Labs 6, 7, and 8. The examples pictured use simple spray paint.
3. Adhere your design onto the steel.
4. Etch the design in the ferric chloride.
5. Clean off acid when you achieve your desired depth.
6. Hammer pieces of prepared metal against your new, clean texture plate.

Experiment

The sky's the limit with the texture options available. The thick plates you created for this lab should last you awhile without wearing down.

Examples of copper and silver hammered against etched steel

Tip

If you have trouble holding the plate while you hammer, anchor it to a large piece of wood or an old sturdy table by screwing it down. No need to drill holes in the steel plate. The screws will hold if you use four or more and place them half on the steel plate, around the plate's edge. Be sure to keep your plate oiled so it won't rust.

Rolling
with the Flow

ROLLING MILLS—tools that allow you to flatten or impress designs onto metal or make thicker metal thinner—are great fun in the studio. Much like with an old ringer washer, metal—alone or with material such as leaves or lace—gets fed between two rollers of a mill for flattening or to create an impression. Mills typically come with grooved rollers (for making and forging down wire) and flat rollers. The labs in this book deal with the latter. Though rolling mills can cost a pretty penny, with a little searching you may find a reasonably inexpensive one that's two to three inches (5.1 to 7.6 cm) wide.

Once you have a rolling mill, it's important to properly care for it. Never roll steel objects through the mill without extra protection such as sheets of brass around it, or you risk damaging the rollers. Instead, sandwich your metal and your object between two brass sheets, and then roll through. Also, always roll dried materials; moisture will rust and cause holes on the rollers.

Roll your design first, and then saw it out. If you do it in reverse order, the roll mill will distort your design. When you feed material into the mill, test the edge to decide how much pressure you need. Poke your metal between the rollers and start turning the handle; you should be able to turn it without too much force. If it's difficult to turn, back out the sandwich and loosen the pressure. (You don't want it to get stuck between the rollers.) With too much pressure your material will distort; too little and you won't get an imprint.

Opposite page: *For this unit, a rolling mill such as the one shown here is key.*
Opposite page (inset): *A sterling roll-mill patterned ring by Sara Westermark*

UNIT 3

In this lesson, we roll natural objects such as leaves and insect wings to imprint the metal's surface. It's amazing just what can leave its mark on the metal when placed under pressure.

- metal
- dry, flat, natural material such as leaves
- torch
- roll mill

"I must go to Nature disarmed of perspective and stretch myself like a large transparent canvas upon her in the hope that, my submission being perfect, the imprint of a beautiful and useful truth would be taken."

—John Updike, writer

Earrings and bracelets imprinted with ferns

Instructions

Feeding a sandwich of metal and dried leaf into the mill

1. Anneal and flatten your metal.
2. Roll it and your natural object such as a leaf, or an insect wing, through the mill using flat rollers.

Tip

If you tape your object onto the metal, the tape will show. Solution: Make the tape wider than your design. Also, wet leaves don't imprint, but just squish and make a mess. Dry them out in a press or book first.

Experiment

When you are out walking, begin looking for interesting leaves, thin vines, and dried weeds. Wet, green leaves won't imprint, but rather will just squish and make a mess. Keep an old book to flatten and dry them. Try using varying amounts of pressure to achieve the best result.

An assortment of natural items printed onto metal

Materials & Tools

- etched brass plate
- metal
- torch
- roll mill

"Pressure makes diamonds."

—George S. Patton,
U. S. Army general

In this lab, we emboss using designs etched onto thick brass sheets with PNP transfer paper. Use any etching method you choose. Refer back to Labs 7 and 8 for an etching refresher. Once your metal is imprinted with the pattern from the brass you can anneal it and make it into jewelry.

Etched plates rolled through a mill make interesting texture on metal. The pattern on the charm's background was achieved this way.

Instructions

1. Anneal the metal you intend to roll.

2. Feed the brass texture sheet and your annealed metal together into the mill. Roll the two pieces through.

Tip

If you're using text, be sure you reverse it in the etching so that when you roll it, it reads in the correct direction.

Experiment

Other types of etched designs might give you a totally different look. For example, brass sheets etched with spray paint could give an abstract overall texture.

Details of the impressed copper

Using Stickers with a Mill

- metal
- stickers
- sandpaper
- patina
- jump rings
- bracelet
- torch
- roll mill
- disc cutter or bench pin, saw, and blades
- drill
- dapping block
- pliers

"We can do anything we want to if we stick to it long enough."

—Helen Keller, activist and writer

In this lab, we play with stickers to imprint metal put through a roll mill. Flat stickers work best. The stickers leave just their outlines on the metal, so play close attention to their outer shape—not their distracting, beautiful colors—when making your selections.

The charms in this finished bracelet were dapped to dome them, and then reverse-stamped with a center punch to add depth to the flower centers.

Instructions

Stickers imprinted onto metal

1. Anneal the metal you want to roll.
2. Stick on your stickers.
3. Roll the metal through the mill.
4. Chop out each design using a disc cutter, or saw out into charms.
5. Anneal each charm again.
6. Drill holes for jump rings.
7. Dome each charm using a dapping block.
8. Sand and finish the edges, and patina the charms.
9. Attach the charms to a bracelet using pliers and the jump rings.

Tip

For this process, pick flat stickers over those with raised designs. If you want to use other kinds of stickers, remove any spongy material to get them as flat as possible.

Experiment

After you try a few stickers, you'll want to hit the sticker aisle of every store. Go for it! You never know what you'll find. Also try cutting out your own designs from sticker paper, or use a personal cutting machine such as a Cricut, if you have one.

In this lab, we experiment with cut paper to impress designs onto metal. You have many options here, from punched-paper designs to cutting-machine designs to your own scissor work. Also, the paper you choose leaves texture, so experiment with different types.

- paper punches (or cutting-machine cutouts)
- paper
- metal, 18-gauge or thicker
- pickle
- painter's or masking tape or glue
- patina, optional
- scissors, optional
- torch
- roll mill
- shears
- sandpaper or file

Leaves punched out of sandpaper made the bracelet pictured.

Instructions

1. Choose punches and paper from your local hobby store, and punch or cut out designs.

2. Anneal and pickle your metal.

3. Affix your design to the metal using glue or tape wider than your metal. (Tape not wider will print and leave a texture.)

4. Feed your design and metal through the roll mill.

5. Using shears, trim the metal to a size you'd like. For a cuff bracelet, for example, cut the metal into a 6-inch (15.2 cm) strip.

6. Finish the edges by filing or sanding.

7. Anneal and pickle the metal again to make it flexible for shaping.

8. Shape the cuff. You should be able to bend it into shape, or use a soft mallet and a bracelet form, if you have one. Then patina and buff it.

Tip

Don't use too much pressure. It can warp your paper-punched designs. Just a slight bit of pressure will leave an imprint. Try a few first before you begin on your final piece of metal.

Experiment

The paper you choose will also leave a texture, so experiment with different types. Sandpaper leaves a nice texture. It was used on the cuff shown on the opposite page. As in the bracelet pictured, think about sawing out portions of your design to punctuate the silhouettes.

Painter's tape covered the metal and cutouts as they went through the roll mill.

Commercial Stampings

Thin, lacy brass stampings or thin brass stencils from the hobby story will go through the mill and can leave lovely patterns on your metal. Design jewelry or metal objects using the lacy imprinted metal. This is a great way to get your favorite brass stamping design imprinted onto silver.

- thin brass stampings, store-bought
- metal
- packing tape, optional
- torch
- roll mill
- shears

"Courage is grace under pressure."

—Ernest Hemingway, writer

A necklace made with metal rolled with a brass stamp piece

Instructions

An inexpensive stamping rolled onto sterling silver

1. Anneal the metal you want to roll.
2. Feed your metal through the mill with the brass stamped piece. Either hold it with your hands or tape it down. Note, however, that tape will leave a mark.
3. Cut out the designed metal and use it in a piece of jewelry.

Tip

Sometimes you can get more than one use out of these brass stampings, but not always. It is possible to anneal brass stampings after rolling, but they cannot take much heat and melt easily. Once heated, allow the piece to cool on its own; *don't quench it*. Then you should be able to roll it through again.

Experiment

The impression you get is the opposite of the stamping. What would happen if you rolled an impressed piece, layered along with the stamping, back through the mill on a new piece of metal? The roll mill also can pattern leather and matt board, which could open up a world of new possibilities!

Brass stamps coming through the roll mill. You don't need to affix them to the metal before rolling.

Forming

WHEN DESIGNING JEWELRY and small metal pieces, adding dimension takes your artwork from mundane and pizza-like—flat with other flat objects on top—to intriguing and sculptural. Learning to use form adds so much to your metalworking repertoire. Once you grasp the concept, you can begin to imagine how you might use some of the forms in the following labs.

Floral form by Kathryn Osgood

Making fold-form Leaves

- roofing copper or 24-gauge copper
- bowl of water
- torch
- shears or snips
- hammers
- small anvil or metal block
- clam or oyster knife

"Nature does not hurry, yet everything is accomplished."

—Lao Tzu,
Taoist philosopher

You can push metal by controlling how much force you use and where you use it. In this exercise, you fold metal much like origami, but you curve it with hammer blows. A hammer with a wedge-shaped peen, such as a bordering hammer, a forging hammer, or a riveting hammer, works best. You'll also need a way to anneal the metal and a clam or oyster knife for opening the forms.

Earrings and leaves made by fold forming

Instructions

Cut out a half circle from the folded-over metal. This is what you will hammer.

Using an oyster or clam knife, pry open the formed metal. It should curve and arch back as you open it.

1. Fold your metal in half, and then use shears to cut out a half-circle in the shape of a taco. You can anneal before you fold, if you like.

2. Anneal the half-circle of folded metal. Quench if you're using copper or silver.

3. Hammer *only* along the curved seam of your half-circle. Make repeated blows along the opening. You should begin to see the metal curl and curve. Do not hammer along the straight, folded edge.

Tip

Angle the hammer to get a better curve. A slight curve to the hammer peen will help as well. And hold the hammer farther back on the handle. This allows for economy of force. Finally, if the metal piece is really small, use pliers or tweezers to hold it as you hammer.

Experiment

Learn to control your hammer blows. Apply different levels of pressure to find the best force to achieve the curve you want. Enhance ruffling with pliers or by hammering only in sections. You might also try different metal thicknesses for different results. And try different sizes of the folded taco shape. In fact, starting larger may be helpful.

4. Anneal the newly shaped metal. Again, quench if using copper or silver.

5. With a blunt-ended knife, pry open the form like you would a clamshell. If you have hammered and annealed the form properly, it should curve and arch back as you open it.

The dark marks on the form indicate spots for hammering to achieve ruffles.

16 Making Fold-Form Boats

Materials & Tools

- roofing copper or 24-gauge copper
- bowl of water
- torch
- shears or snips
- hammers
- small anvil or metal block
- clam or oyster knife

"The anvil is not afraid of the hammer."

—Charles Spurgeon, preacher

Much like in Lab 15, here we experiment with controlled deformation of metal. This time though, we hammer the straight, folded edge of our metal rather than the curved open side. Watch as this change creates a different form.

Jewelry like these boat-shaped earrings comes from folding and hammering.

Instructions

Hammering along the straight, folded edge of a half-circle of metal produces pod-shaped fold forms like these.

1. Fold your metal in half, and then use shears to cut out a half-circle in the shape of a taco. You can anneal before you fold, if you like.

2. Anneal the half-circle of metal. Quench if you're using copper or silver.

3. Hammer *only* along the spine or closed, folded edge of the half-circle. Make repeated blows up the spine. You should begin to see the metal curl and curve. Do not hammer along the open, curved side.

4. Anneal the newly shaped metal. Again, quench if using copper or silver.

5. With a blunt-ended knife, pry open the form like you would a clamshell. If you have hammered and annealed the form properly, it will shape into a canoe as you open it.

Hammering along the straight, folded edge of a half-circle of metal produces pod-shaped fold forms like these.

- roofing copper or 22-gauge copper, cut into a 6-inch (15.2 cm) strip
- bowl of water
- wet/dry sandpaper
- patina
- clear sealant or shellac, optional
- shears or snips
- torch
- hammers
- small anvil or metal block
- clam or oyster knife
- file
- pliers, optional
- saw, optional

In this lesson, we expand on the use of fold-forming to make a cuff bracelet. The metal curls around further as you open the hammered form.

Finished cuffs made by fold-forming metal

Instructions

The three metal pieces, from top to bottom: A metal strip annealed, pickled, folded in half, and then cut into a long half-leaf shape with an open seam on a curved edge. To the left sits a metal strip hammered into a curve ready to be opened into a cuff.

1. Cut a 6-inch (15.2 cm) piece of metal to fold.

2. Fold your metal in half, and then cut it into an elongated half-circle. You can anneal before you fold, if you like.

3. Anneal the elongated half-circle. Quench if you're using copper or silver.

4. Choose where you hammer. Either hammer *only* along the spine or closed edge of your half-circle shape or *only* on the open seam. Make repeated blows. You should begin to see the metal curl and curve. Anneal and repeat hammering to achieve a slight horseshoe shape. Once you arrive at the horseshoe shape, stop. The metal will curl more as you pry it open.

Tip

If you open your form and it's not satisfactory, refold it and continue hammering. Be sure you anneal to avoid cracking. Also, try making multiple cuffs. The more you do, the better you will become at judging how much more it will curve as it opens.

Experiment

In this lab we hammered only on the folded edge or spine of the form. Try hammering the curved, open side the next time. The bracelets pictured are each hammered on differing edges, which achieves opposite results.

5. Anneal the newly shaped metal.

6. With a blunt-ended knife, pry open the form like you would a clamshell. If you have hammered and annealed the form properly, it will shape into a canoe or curve and arch back, depending on which side you hammered.

7. File and sand the bracelet's edges. Address the two ends by folding over the material, curling it with pliers, or sawing off any excess. Be sure you sand and smooth it.

8. Finish with patina or spray such as clear sealant or shellac.

Opening a hammered curve to make a cuff. The metal will curl more as you open it.

Form to Die For

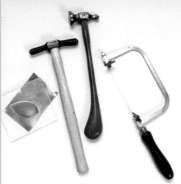

Here we add dimension to metal by slightly puffing the sheet, done by hammering from the backside of the annealed metal. Metal 20- to 24-gauge works best for this technique. Use Plexiglas or medium density fiberboard (MDF) for the dies into which you will hammer.

Plexiglas can sometimes be tedious to cut. You need spiral or 'skip-a-tooth' blades made for cutting wax or plastic. If you decide to try Plexiglas, take your time, wax your blade, and find a rhythm. Sawing Plexi too quickly can melt the plastic behind the blade, and going too slowly can get the blade stuck. Find the speed that is just right.

- cardstock
- copper or silver, 20- or 24-gauge
- Plexiglas or MDF, ¼-inch (6 mm) thick
- scissors
- drill and bits
- saw blades, spiral or skip-a-tooth
- jeweler's saw
- file
- torch
- hammers

To create this form, copper was hammered into a circular depression in Plexiglas and then sawn in half.

Instructions

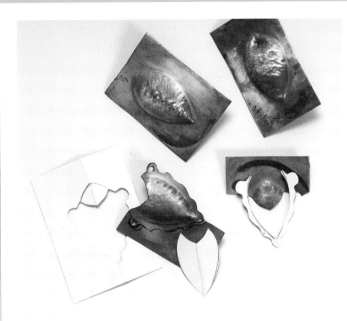

Draw designs on an index card, which you can cut out and trace.

1. Choose a design for your form. Simple shapes work best.
2. Draw your design on cardstock and cut it out.
3. Trace the cut-out design onto your plastic or MDF.
4. Inside your drawn line, drill a small hole big enough to thread your saw blade through.
5. Saw out the drawn shape in the board.
6. File the edges of your form, if needed, to refine its shape.

Tip

If you're using MDF, try drilling holes and screwing your metal to the form. Bolt or tape it into place if you're using Plexiglas.

Experiment

Try different hammers to achieve different textures. If you need to, stop and anneal your metal numerous times until you get the desired shape. The necklace pictured was sawn after it was hammered. It was also embellished with punches.

7. Lay annealed metal *larger* than your shape over the hole you sawed. It needs to exceed the size of the hole so you can hold onto it.
8. Choose a hammer. With one hand holding the metal, begin hammering from the backside, pushing the metal into the cavity of your sawn-out shape.
9. Lay your puffed piece of metal face up and saw off the outer border.
10. File and sand the edges, and incorporate it into a piece of jewelry.

Hammering into the form with a rounded hammer

Making Connections

UNIT 5

IN THIS UNIT, we explore ways to connect metal to other objects without using heat. Such connections are often called *cold connections* or *cold joins*. The rivet is the most used of these techniques. Rivets come in many guises, but we work with two basic ones and one commercial type.

One of the best aspects of cold connections is that you can join things that cannot take heat; and if you have a drill, some wire, a metal surface, and a hammer, you can make almost anything!

Enameled and riveted bracelets by Kate Cathey

Tube Rivets

- tubing
- metal shapes
- tape, optional
- sliding millimeter gauge
- dapping punches or conical transfer punches
- drill or hole punch, same diameter as tubing
- round-needle file
- pliers
- jig, optional
- metal bench block
- scribe or Sharpie pen
- jeweler's saw
- hammer

"True happiness comes from the joy of deeds well done, the zest of creating things new."

—Antoine de Saint-Exupéry, aviator and writer

Tube rivets are connections made out of small, thin tubing. In this lab, we drill holes through a sandwich of materials we intend to join, large enough to accept a little slice of tube. We then flare that tube on either side of our metal sandwich and it holds together the pieces with no soldering, much like a grommet or eyelet.

Metal pieces joined together using tube rivets

Instructions

A punch is used to flare out the tubing to make a rivet.

1. Use the sliding **millimeter gauge** to make sure your drill bit or punch matches your tubing. There is a sizing chart in the back of this book for your convenience. Make a test hole in scrap metal to be sure.

2. Drill a hole into your top piece of metal, align it with your bottom sheet, and then punch or drill the hole all the way through. If the pieces won't stay aligned, tape or clamp them together.

3. File the hole with the round-needle file, if needed. Don't overfile! The tubing (which you'll soon put in) must sit snugly in the hole.

4. Align the two pieces of metal on a block, and insert the tubing into the hole. Scribe or mark the tubing where it sticks out of the hole on either side, allowing an amount equal to half the tube's diameter to stick up out of the hole. This is really only a smidge on either side for a successful rivet.

Tip

If you want movement—with a rotating arrow spinner, for example—insert paper in between the sandwich layers while you're connecting the two, and then pull or soak it out later. Also, if you don't have a tubing cutter or jig, take a coarse, small round file and file a trough on top of your bench pin into which you'll lay the tubing as you saw. This keeps it from rolling around too much.

Experiment

Visualizing half the diameter of the tubing is sometimes difficult. Through experimenting, you'll learn to know how much is too much or not enough. Usually, all you need is the width of two or three extra-fine-point Sharpie marks.

5. Remove the tubing from the hole and saw it at your mark.

6. Gently file off the burr, if needed, and insert the tubing back into your holes.

7. Set your piece onto a metal block and place the tip of a punch into the tube. While holding the punch with one hand, gently tap it with a hammer. This flares the tubing just a tad. Flip over the whole piece, holding the tubing in place as you flip, and repeat the process on the other side.

8. Flip over the piece numerous times, working between front and back, to set the rivet tight and until the tubing has flattened on both sides, like eyelets.

Tube-cutting pliers and jigs make cutting the tube easier.

Standard Rivets

- wire
- metal shapes
- tape, optional
- sliding millimeter gauge
- drill bit the same diameter as the wire
- drill
- metal bench block
- small hammer (French riveting or chasing)
- flush-cutting pliers
- torch, optional

Standard rivets are similar to tube rivets in that we use them to join together a sandwich of metal and other materials. But here's the difference: Standard rivets do not have a hole. Rather, they are often like little nails. In fact you could rivet with tiny brass nails if you wanted. In this lab, we use copper or silver wire to make our own little rivets.

Standard rivets connect layers on these charms

Instructions

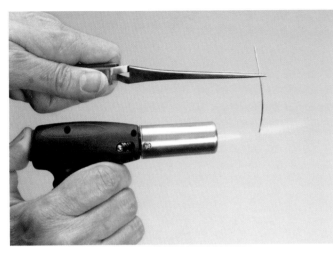

Balling the end of a wire with a torch

1. Use the sliding millimeter gauge to make sure your drill bit matches your wire. (You also can drill a test hole in scrap metal.) A hole that is too big will cause a loose rivet that flops over and looks awful.

2. Drill a hole into the top sheet of metal, align it with your bottom sheet, and then drill the hole all the way through. If the pieces won't stay aligned, tape or clamp them together.

3. Lay the sandwich of metal on a metal block and insert the wire into the hole.

4. Flush cut the wire using flush-cutting pliers, leaving a small, even nub to hammer. Leaving too much wire causes your rivet to flop over.

Tip

Make a little "headpin" to rivet by first balling wire with a torch, then hammering it flat in a rivet block. Half your work is finished in no time!

Experiment

As with the tube rivet, you need half the diameter of the rivet sticking out of each side. This is sometimes difficult to visualize. Again, through experimenting, you'll learn to know how much is too much or not enough. Usually, all you need is the width of two or three extra-fine-point-Sharpie marks.

5. Hammer the exposed wire gently, though—important—don't yet flush it against the metal. If using a chasing hammer, use the round end.

6. Flip over the whole sandwich on the metal block and push down, exposing some of the wire.

7. Hammer the exposed wire flush. Flip it back over to see whether you need to hammer more on the back. A small, rounded hammer will mushroom the rivet over the edge.

Flatten it with a hammer to create a headpin to rivet.

Cold-Joining Plastics

Materials & Tools

- metal, 22-gauge or thicker
- Plexiglas, ⅛-inch (3 mm) sheet
- wet/dry sandpaper
- beeswax or jeweler's cut lube
- tubing
- tape, optional
- jeweler's saw
- 3/0 saw blades
- files
- drill
- drill bit that matches tubing
- metal block
- punch
- hammer

"Creativity is the power to connect the seemingly unconnected."

—William Plomer, writer

Plexiglas and other plastics can be easily joined to metal with rivets. In this exercise, we opt for tube rivets, as in Lab 19. Think creatively and you'll come up with other plastics that would work with metal such as toothbrush handles or parts from children's toys.

Design and function merge as the sawn silver piece behind the plastic also acts as a washer.

Instructions

1. Determine your pattern. Trace it onto your metal and then trace a design onto your plastic.

2. Saw out the metal, and then file and sand the edges.

3. Saw out the plastic shape, then file and sand the edges. (See Lab 18 for details about sawing Plexiglas.)

4. Make sure your drill bit matches your tubing, then drill holes into the top piece.

5. Tape or clamp together your pieces, if necessary, then drill one hole all the way through both.

6. Insert your tubing into the hole on a metal block and measure.

7. Cut your tubing to size.

8. Insert the cut tube rivet back into the hole and set your rivet. (See Lab 19 for detailed instructions on this.)

9. Repeat the process for the second rivet.

Tip

Leave the protective film on your Plexiglas as long as possible to avoid scratching its surface.

Experiment

Remember, Plexiglas is translucent, so have fun with that fact and make pieces that take advantage of it. Also, you can sand Plexiglas for a foggy, translucent look. See the dirigible necklace in Lab 7.

Colored Plexiglas can result in fun, beautiful pieces.

Recycling Tin

Tins are all around us. In this lab, we cut them open and use them as material, much like a patchwork quilt. First, you need to make a cardstock pattern; a manila folder and tape or a small cereal box work well for this. You may even decide to start with a project simpler than the backpack shown. One important note: Tin is sharp so wear gloves when handling it!

- tins
- wire
- headpin rivets
- pop rivets
- wet/dry sandpaper
- tin snips and shears
- gloves
- drill or hole punch
- drill bit to match wire
- rivet gun
- hammer
- metal block
- rawhide or plastic mallet, optional

This tin backpack uses a store-bought hinge as a closure.

Instructions

These straps were made from Boy Scout belts. The pewter buckles were embellished with riveted tin.

1. While wearing gloves, cut open any kind of tin boxes—carefully—and trim off sharp points from the tin and crimps from bottle caps.

2. Create a large sheet like a quilt by riveting pieces together with small or headpin rivets. Make sheets to fit your pattern. (See Lab 20 for detailed instructions on making rivets.)

3. Cut out pieces from your quilt sheets to form into walls.

4. Plan and pre-punch holes in the sheets to join together the walls.

5. Join together the larger pieces using a rivet gun and pop rivets. (See Lab 25 for more detail.)

Experiment

You can easily rivet tin pieces to other objects such as wood boxes, leather, or book covers. Tin makes a great jewelry embellishment. Refer back to the charms in the previous riveting labs.

Tin comes in many shapes and sizes, from tintypes to bottle caps.

Tip

Shears will leave a burr on the tin's edge. When possible, cut the tin so the burr lands on the inside of an edge that will be riveted down. You also can sand edges a bit, but the best defense against a sharp edge is to fold it over and pound it flat with a rawhide or plastic mallet.

23 Recycling Street Signs

Street signs make great found metal. They are made of thick aluminum easily cut with a jeweler's saw. Don't steal the signs, but rather check with your local recycling facility for leftovers. You also need to cut them into usable pieces with a jigsaw, band saw, or jump shears. (A metal shop also could cut them up for you.) The signs' vibrant colors and reflective paint give your pieces a contemporary, urban flair.

- road sign pieces
- wet/dry sandpaper
- ear wires
- jeweler's saw
- #0 saw blades
- file
- drill
- drill bits

"In the right light, at the right time, everything is extraordinary."

—Aaron Rose, director

Road sign earrings made by Nick Mowers

Instructions

1. Saw out matching shapes from street signs.
2. File down rough edges.
3. Sand edges.
4. Drill holes and attach ear wires.

Tip

The dust from aluminum filings can be hazardous to breathe in, and the filings can be flammable, so clean up after yourself! And please do our environment a favor: Don't toss aluminum scraps in the trash. Instead, return them to your recycling facility with your cans.

Experiment

Try partially drilling into the sign or filing into it to reveal silvery aluminum.

Road sign aluminum can be cut into nearly any shape.

Hobby suppliers sell micro or miniature nuts and bolts. These little parts come with matching washers in a few different sizes. They usually arrive with a matching driver that looks like a blunt center punch. Mini bolts make fabulous, easy fasteners for jewelry and can result in a great Machine Age look.

- metal
- miniature nuts and bolts
- matching driver for the nuts
- drill or hole punch
- drill bit to match mini bolts

"We must walk consciously only part way toward our goal, and then leap in the dark to our success."

—Henry David Thoreau, naturalist, writer, and philosopher

Mini bolts can make a piece of jewelry look like it's from the Machine Age.

Instructions

1. Plan out your design and drill holes accordingly.
2. Insert a mini bolt into a hole.
3. Screw on the washer and nut onto the backside, using the matching driver.
4. Repeat until you fill all of your holes.

Tip

To permanently adhere the nut, apply epoxy or commercial "lock tight." Or take a center punch and dent the bolt in the middle of the nut. This will flare the bolt a little like a rivet, and your nut will never come off.

Experiment

To allow for a wider sandwich of materials, try different length bolts.

Miniature bolts work well when joining objects such as plastic that cannot take heat.

Pop Rivets

Pop rivets are an easy way to connect materials. They're available through most hardware stores in a variety of sizes and diameters. They are aluminum so they don't take a lot of stress or wear and tear, but they can provide instant gratification.

- materials to connect
- pop rivets
- hole punch or drill
- drill bits to match rivets
- pop rivet gun

"Better a little which is well done, than a great deal imperfectly."
—Plato, Greek philosopher

Pop rivets join this antique keyhole with a tintype to copper.

Instructions

1. Plan out your design and punch or drill holes to match the rivets.

2. Align the material you plan to rivet.

3. Insert the fatter end of the rivet into the first hole. With rivet in place, insert the skinny end of the rivet into the gun tip. (You also can reverse these two steps and start with the rivet in the gun.)

4. Squeeze the handle of the gun together multiple times. Pressure will build up and the stem of the rivet will "pop" off, leaving the rivet in your material.

5. Discard the stem by releasing the gun handle.

Tip

If you have a thick material to join, look for rivets with longer stems.

Experiment

Pop rivets, by their nature, look very commercial. Try giving them a handmade look by hammering them slightly. Or punch the stem out of the middle of an already set rivet, giving it the appearance of a tube rivet. Hammer it slightly for texture. Pop rivets also come in different colors and with wider faces.

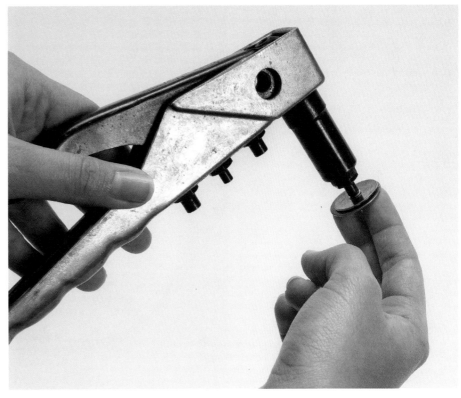

Using a pop rivet gun to fasten a pop rivet

Materials & Tools

- metal
- wet/dry sandpaper
- objects to trap
- jeweler's saw
- #3/0 saw blades
- needle files
- scribe
- drill
- drill bits

"Failure is simply an opportunity to begin again, this time more intelligently."

—Henry Ford, founder of Ford Motor Company

Metal tabs—like the little pieces of paper that stick out from the edge of a paper doll's dress—are fantastic tools to trap objects onto metal. They function much like fingers and can be attached to or sawn directly out of the surrounding metal.

A shell is held in place with skinny pronglike tabs (see the shell necklace). And a steel square is fastened to silver with tabs (bottom).

Instructions

Tabs are sawn out of the design to hold a wooden lotto coin.

1. Saw from the metal a pendant or charm big enough to attach an object to. File and sand the edges.

2. Trace with a scribe the object you plan to enclose onto the charm.

3. Plan out where to place the tabs and draw them on the traced area with a scribe. Leave extra metal as a lip under the object so it doesn't fall out the backside.

4. Drill a hole somewhere in the middle to access the tabs.

5. Saw out the tabs a little past the edge of the traced object mark. This will account for the object's thickness.

6. Bend up tabs and test whether the object fits between them.

7. Sand or finish the edges with a file, if needed.

Experiment

Get creative with the metal that remains on the backside to hold in your object. You could give it a decorative edge. Also, your tabs can be elaborate shapes; they don't have to be square or plain. Notice the curled tabs in the washer brooches.

Brooches using tabs to connect washers, lenses, and metal by Melissa Manley

Tip

Be sure to texture the metal before you saw out your tabs. Hammering after the fact will distort your metal and your object may not fit.

Materials & Tools

- metal
- wet/dry sandpaper
- index card
- tape
- metal tubing or rivets
- objects to trap, such as pebbles
- jeweler's saw
- #2/0 saw blades
- round-needle file
- dapping punch
- drill or hole punch
- drill bits
- metal block

Trapping objects with straps or domed metal pieces is an exciting way to use materials that cannot take the heat that soldering requires. The complexities of cold-connecting these materials can cause you to think more creatively about construction. Here rivets hold together the metal pieces.

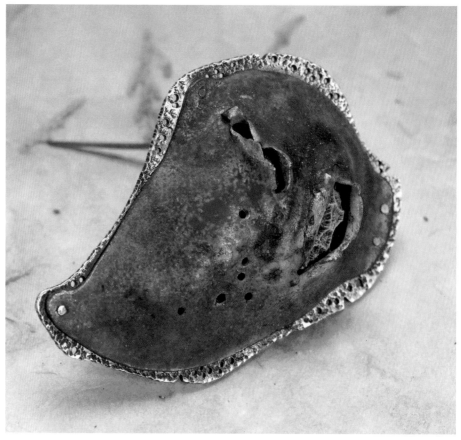

In this brooch, fossilized coral is trapped under a domed piece of enameled copper.

"Here we are, trapped in the amber of the moment. There is no why."

— Kurt Vonnegut, writer

Instructions

Half the fun is collecting objects to trap, such as these bottle caps and rocks.

1. Saw out of metal a shape to which you can attach an object. File and sand the edges.

2. On an index card, draw a pattern of the strap you'd like to make over your object.

3. Trace the pattern you just made onto a piece of metal and saw it out. Finish edges.

4. Punch or drill holes where the strap needs rivets.

5. Tape your strap onto the metal, and using the strap as a guide, mark where your first rivet needs to go on your background piece. Drill that hole through the background.

Tip

You may need an extra hand to rivet unusual shapes. Find a buddy to hold the metal while you set the rivet. Also, drilling a hole first in the top layer, then consecutively in the background layer, will help you keep holes aligned. If you drill all holes through everything and then try to rivet, you will run into alignment issues.

Experiment

Get creative with what you use as a metal support under your rivet; flat blocks may not always work. Polished train spikes make good curved "anvils" when clamped in a small vise.

6. Insert your object under the strap to begin riveting. Again, consider using tape to hold the object in place.

7. Set the first rivet only. (See Labs 19 and 20 for detailed instructions on how to do this.)

8. Drill your next hole all the way through the background piece and set the next rivet. File the hole first with a round-needle file, if needed, to get the rivet snugly through all layers.

9. Drill remaining holes and set remaining rivets.

This belt buckle traps stones from opposite coasts.

Soldering

JEWELER'S SOLDER MELTS at much higher temperatures than plumber or stained-glass solder, and is composed of either silver or gold and other metals with specific melting points. When purchasing solder—which comes in little chips called **pallions**, as wire, or as a sheet—you'll select your material based on melting point. *Easy*, *medium*, and *hard* are your most common options.

Different melting points allow a jeweler to have various solder joints on a single piece of jewelry. Easy flows at 1,325°F (718°C), medium flows at 1,360°F (738°C), and hard flows at 1,450°F (788°C), so if you solder first with the one that melts at the highest melting point, when you solder the next joint, the first one should not come unsoldered. For example, if you solder on a band or to a ring and then need to later solder on decoration or a basket to hold a stone, begin with the hardest solder to melt, move on to medium, and then use the easiest for your final job.

Solder functions only under very specific conditions, the first of which is cleanliness. This makes sense once you understand how solder works. Picture the metal molecules as little bricks. Once heated, the spaces between the metal's bricks expand, creating a place into which other molecules can move. Once allowed to flow in between, solder becomes like mortar. As the heat is removed and cooling begins, everything locks into place—making solder an extremely tight bond when done properly. This is also why jewelers' solder melts at such high temperatures.

UNIT 6

Lower-temperature solders behave more like caulk than bonding cement. Let's go back to the brick example. Obstructions in the space between the bricks prevent the solder from flowing there. So we need to create a protective bubble. This is our **flux**. Flux is a paste or liquid solution that forms a gooey or glasslike coating over the solder and joint to keep out oxidation, allowing solder to flow.

Also, solder does not jump gaps, so make sure your seam has no large open areas, and that everything touches. Solder is a "party animal" and will go to the hottest spot. So if you have a hot, bumping party down the block, it'll stroll on down. In other words, you need to evenly heat your whole project and only zero in on the joint in question when the flux turns glassy and honeylike and the temperature looks right. Pay attention to where you aim your torch so as not to tempt the solder
to run to where you don't want it. Finally, cooler areas act as heat sinks, sucking heat from the joint where you need it. Again, heat the project evenly.

Successful soldering takes practice. You must learn how the metal looks when the solder is about to flow, and this only happens through practice and having your own lightbulb go off. To recap, for a successful solder joint, you need:

- flux
- solder
- a tight joint, where everything that needs soldering
  touches and no light comes through the seams
- even heating
- hot temperatures throughout the whole piece

Solders and fluxes can contain chemicals not safe to breathe. Always do this work where you have some sort of ventilation. Place a fan to draw fumes away from your face—and out an open window. Some easy solders contain cadmium, dangerous to breathe when hot, so check with your supplier. Also, fluxes can contain fluorides which make them function better but are noxious and dangerous to breathe. Find fluoride-free fluxes, when possible, and again, always ventilate.

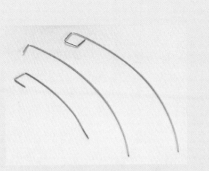

Flux and wired solder that has been keyed. From left to right: medium, easy, and hard.

Soldering tools such as tweezers and tripods make soldering easier. Various heatproof surfaces and blocks are available on the market. Most jewelry-supply catalogs have a variety, along with diagrams showing them in use.

28 I'm with the Band (Ring)

In this lab, we learn how to measure and solder band rings out of metal strips. (For sizes, see the chart in the Resources section of this book.) There are many tools to help making rings easier: marked and unmarked mandrels (those with no engravings on them), half-round forming pliers, ring clamps, and miter jigs (which hold metal while you file a perfect angle), to name a few. Rings are popular and there are always new devices and products on the market that make creating them much easier. And remember Aristotle's words: "Well begun is half done." This is especially true with ring seams.

- sterling metal strip, 3 inches (7.6 cm) or longer
- flux
- solder, easy or medium
- pickle
- wet/dry sandpaper
- millimeter calipers
- shears
- full-size, flat hand file
- half-round ring forming pliers
- paintbrush
- soldering surface
- torch
- rawhide mallet
- metal ring mandrel
- full-size, half-round ring hand file

Textured silver band rings

Instructions

1. Texture your strip of metal.

2. Measure it using a millimeter gauge or the chart in the back of the book. Saw the metal strip so it's the finger millimeters size or corresponding millimeter length you need, based on the chart.

3. File the cut edge of the strip until it's perfectly square and flat.

4. Bend the strip around into a *D* shape using pliers. You'll round it later.

5. Make sure the ends meet in a perfect, tight seam with no light showing through. Keep filing until this happens.

6. Place on a heatproof surface, brush on flux, and place solder.

7. Heat with a torch until flux goes from frothy white to glassy, and the solder flows like mercury. Pull away the torch as soon as the solder flows liquid.

8. Pickle until clean. Rinse well.

9. Round out the ring with a mallet on a metal ring mandrel.

10. Sand the side of the ring with a drop of water on taped-down sandpaper to make the edges even and parallel.

11. File the edges with a half-round file to make the inner edge beveled. Patina and polish as needed.

There are many places to put solder on a ring, such as on top of the seam, seen here.

Solder placed inside on the ring's seam

Experiment

Texture can look great on rings. Experiment with textures before you measure and cut your strip. Doing so after can distort the ring's shape and change its size. Make more than one band ring so you get some practice and the process becomes easier.

Tip

A perfect, tight seam may not happen your first try, so saw your metal strip a hair longer than the chart says. You may have to unbend and file again but this way, you won't lose much length and end up with a ring that's too small. A miter jig can help with filing to achieve a clean seam. If needed, anneal your metal to make it pliable so you can rebend. Pickle it thoroughly before soldering.

Variations of band rings

Stop, Dap, and Trap

- band ring
- pickle
- pen
- felt or other material to trap
- torch
- scissors
- metal block
- dapping punches larger than the ring's diameter
- ball-peen hammer, medium-size
- hard wood surface

"We are shaped and fashioned by what we love."

—Johann Wolfgang von Goethe, author

Dapping and flaring a cylinder or band of metal can trap objects, much like a big grommet (protective eyelet). Thinking about trapping items this way can stretch your imagination and open you up to unconventional methods of joining.

Rings with different trapped objects

Instructions

Using a dapping punch, gently hammer a band ring encircled by felt (as seen here) to flare the band.

1. Anneal the ring until it is soft and pickle clean.

2. With a pen, mark the inner diameter on the felt.

3. Cut the felt into a doughnut or lifesaver shape large enough so the center hole fits over the band ring.

4. Slip the felt doughnut over the band ring.

5. Place the felt-encircled ring on a metal block, and with a large dapping punch and hammer, gently begin to flare the band, hammering once or twice.

6. Flip over the ring, centering the felt, and keep tapping on the opposite sides with the punch and hammer.

7. Repeat gentle tapping on both sides until you achieve your desired effect.

Continue tapping gently on both sides until you reach your desired effect.

Experiment

Try completely smashing down the sides of the ring, like a big grommet. Here are a few experiments to try:

- Saw cuts into the band, then flare it.

- Use different materials trapped between the flared sides of the ring-like beads.

- Experiment with stacking layers of material.

- Cut designs into the felt.

- Trap a ring of a bigger finger size so that it won't come off, but is allowed to spin.

Tip

Don't bottom out with the punch on the metal block. If you are, you'll hear a metallic "clack" as the punch hits the block. Stop! You don't want to flatten the tip of your round punch. If you have a larger punch, now's the time to move up to the next size.

Sweat Soldering

- metal
- sawn out design
- flux
- solder
- pickle
- wet/dry sandpaper
- masking tape
- jeweler's saw
- paintbrush
- soldering surface
- torch

"The cure for anything is salt water. In one way or the other; sweat, tears, or the salt sea."

—Isak Dinesen, writer

The method of sweat soldering adheres together flat sawn designs. Solder is melted in hundreds of tiny polka dots on the back of a design, like beads of sweat, then the decorative piece is sanded and then soldered onto the background.

This silhouetted figure was sweat-soldered onto the metal background to create a beautiful necklace.

Instructions

Sand the little hills of solder with a drop of water before soldering it to your background.

1. Saw and finish your two metal pieces. Clean thoroughly the one that will become the top design.
2. Lay your sawn design face down and brush on flux. Lay down multiple solder pallions, like polka dots, all over the back on top of the flux.
3. Heat until the solder dots melt and puddle.
4. Pickle until clean and rinse.
5. Lay the design solder-side down onto taped-down sandpaper. Add a drop of water and sand the solder until it is level.
6. Rinse clean and paint on another layer of flux.
7. Lay your background face up on your working surface, paint on flux, then add the design, face up, solder-side down onto the background.
8. Begin to warm the pieces of metal. Heat slowly so they don't bubble, steam, and slip out of alignment. Heat until the solder flows; watch for it around the edge.

Experiment

Soldering together metals of different colors, or learning first on copper, can help you see your mistakes.

The silhouette on the left has solder dots partially melted on the back. In the one on the right, the dots have been melted and partially sanded.

Tip

The solder will sometimes be like tiny hills, but sanding will level these out and get rid of any excess. This allows you to solder the design down with minimal spills or blooms of solder seeping out.

Hollow Forms from Domes

Materials & Tools

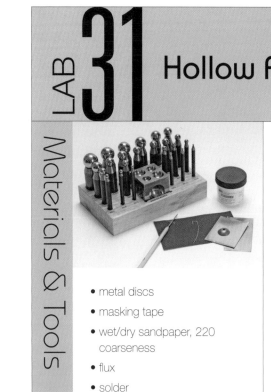

- metal discs
- masking tape
- wet/dry sandpaper, 220 coarseness
- flux
- solder
- pickle
- patina, optional
- torch
- dapping punch set
- dapping block
- metal block
- hammer
- jeweler's saw
- saw blades

In this lab, learn to compose three-dimensional forms by soldering together dome shapes. This is a more challenging lesson than some of the previous lessons, but can be very rewarding. Patience and a little ingenuity go a long way in this process. You'll be soldering together the domes, and then sawing them apart laterally. Because of their size and shape, they can be difficult to hold onto.

Jewelry made from sawn and soldered domes

Instructions

Sanding on taped-down wet/dry sandpaper achieves beautiful, easier-to-solder edges.

1. Anneal discs so they are pliable. You can re-anneal as many times as necessary.

2. Dome discs in dapping block with punches. Don't make them very plump, round forms. You want to end up with saucer shapes.

3. Sand the half domes with a drop or two of water on taped-down sandpaper. Rinse thoroughly.

4. Flux and solder together the half domes. Get innovative in figuring out what tools you can use to hold them together, such as insulated tweezers, or make a slight depression in a charcoal block in which to nest the bottom half.

5. Once the dome cools, saw the dome apart in the opposite direction you soldered together the pieces, creating pods. This won't be easy! Go slowly and be patient.

6. Pickle and sand the sawn form on the sandpaper, if needed. Also, file and sand off solder that has spilled on to the outside.

7. Finish and patina as desired.

Experiment

Get innovative when figuring out which tools you have that can hold the pieces together as you solder, such as insulated tweezers, or make a slight depression in a charcoal block in which to nest the bottom half. Play around with how you saw the forms apart. Some of the earrings shown have attached ear wires loose in a drilled hole; others have ear wires soldered in place. If you don't want to saw the forms, punch holes before you solder and you have a bead!

Tip

You can keep moving the disc around in the dapping block depression and dapping with the punch until you get an even shape. However, keep in mind that these forms are more interesting if they are *not* fully rounded. Too round and the exercise is pointless.

Examples of variations of dome constructions

- copper pipe
- wet/dry sandpaper, 220 coarseness
- masking tape
- flux
- solder, easy and medium
- ring, optional
- bail, optional
- patina, optional
- full-sized, flat hand file
- dividers
- pipe cutter
- soldering tools
- torch

"Your current safe boundaries were once unknown frontiers."

—Anonymous

Round **bezels**, loops of metal, can hold an infinite variety of objects. Once dedicated solely to holding stones, these little round fences now act as barriers for resin, glass, ceramic, putty, grout—the list goes on. Traditional silver bezels are made just like little band rings and use silver bezel strip. For this lab, we play with copper pipe, which is readily available and inexpensive. A tool called a divider will help in marking your metal in this lab. It has two long legs and a wing nut at the apex so it can be moved to the desired width. The points at the leg tips scribe even increments on your metal.

Using copper pipe, create bezel-topped rings like the ones shown here.

Instructions

Place solder, along with flux, inside the pipe touching both the floor and the wall.

Get creative with round bezels, like in this brooch made from a fork.

1. With a file, flatten the wall at the top of the pipe so you have one flat edge on your bezel.

2. Set the divider legs at the height you want your bezel.

3. Place one leg along the top edge of the pipe, and with the bottom leg, scribe a line around the pipe's circumference.

4. Tighten the pipe cutter around the pipe so its wheel sits on the scribed line and there is slight tension.

5. Twist the cutter around the pipe, deeply scribing with the wheel. Give the cutter a slight tightening twist with each pass around the pipe until it cuts through cleanly.

6. Inspect the flat edge you created in step 1. Sand it flat and smooth with a drop of water on 220 wet/dry sandpaper taped down to a flat surface. Rinse it clean.

7. Place your bezel onto a clean, metal background or disc, fluxing both.

8. Place medium solder at even intervals along the wall, touching both the floor and wall.

9. Heat slowly until flux goes glassy and flows.

10. Attach a ring or bail using easy solder. Pickle thoroughly and rinse.

11. Finish and patina as desired.

Experiment

Try sawing bezels to make little tabs to hold in materials.

Tip

If using resin, be sure your solder flows thoroughly and doesn't leave gaps because the resin will seep out. If you find holes, pickle, rinse, flux, and flow solder again. Also, remember to patina and buff completely before you set your stone or resin.

Square Bezels

- 2 metal strips
- flux
- solder
- wet/dry sandpaper
- masking tape
- dividers
- precision square
- C-clamp
- triangular needle file
- square needle files
- soldering surface
- metal ruler
- torch

"Sometimes you have to let go to see if there was anything worth holding on to." —Anonymous

Like round bezels, square ones can hold all kinds of objects, though they're slightly more complicated because they require precise measuring to achieve symmetry. With helpful tools and practice, these bezels will become old hat in no time.

Silver, resin, and mammoth ivory earrings by Nick Mowers

Instructions

The V-shaped groove allows you to achieve a sharp bend at the corner.

1. Determine the size of square needed, then use the dividers and **precision square** to mark lines for one wall.
2. Clamp down your metal strip along the edge of a table.
3. Groove a notch at the edge on your marked line with one of the pointed edges of a triangular file. Keep making a sawing motion, back and forth with the file, as you slowly lower the tip. You will change the angle of your file, making a longer and longer V-shaped trough perpendicularly across the strip of metal. Try to stay on the line so you stay square, making a 90-degree groove.

Tip

Make sure both short legs of each *L* measure the same length (the long side doesn't matter). And be sure they have flat, straight ends that align with the wall neatly. When soldering them together, you can wire them with iron binding wire or pin them tightly in place with quilter's T-pins pushed into a solder brick.

Experiment

Every shape you make doesn't have to be precise. If you measure slightly incorrectly, you may end up with a trapezoid—and a new, fun direction! Also, try making soft, rounded corners on your squares by not scoring with the file. Simply bend them with pliers.

4. File this groove until you think you're about to saw through. You should see a faint line on the backside of the metal. Bend at the groove.
5. Repeat this sequence on a second strip. This makes two Ls that you will solder together to make a square.
6. Flip the *Ls* opposite of one another on a soldering block and push them together.
7. Flux the corners and flow solder down all four.
8. Sand on taped-down sandpaper with a drop of water, then solder these walls to a floor much like the round bezel.

The two short sides should be the same length; saw off the excess metal on the long sides after you finish soldering.

Simple Hinge

Materials & Tools

- index card
- metal
- thick metal rod or tubing
- scissors
- scribe
- dividers
- jeweler's saw
- saw blades
- round pliers
- needle files
- metal block
- hammer

"Whatever good things we build end up building us."

—Jim Rohn,
business philosopher

There are dozens of ways to make hinges. The one in this lab consists of fingerlike strips sawn out of a sheet. Like the tines on a fork, they are bent around a thick rod riveted on both ends to keep it in. The tines function as the hinge's knuckles. Careful planning always helps with hinge-making, so create paper patterns first whenever possible. It will save you from making mistakes on metal that cost both time and money.

The hinge holding this necklace's pendant in place comes from fingerlike pieces sawn out of a metal sheet and then curled in.

Instructions

A strip partially curled into a knuckle

1. Draw a pattern of your design on an index card. Cut it out.
2. Trace the design onto your metal with a scribe. Use dividers to keep even the strips that will become the knuckles.
3. Saw out your design.
4. Curl up your hinge knuckles using round pliers. If they don't fit between each other, file as needed.
5. Measure the rod and cut it the length of your hinge.
6. Insert the rod and rivet either end using a hammer on a metal block.

Tip

The strips of metal in the examples are long. Consider shortening them to make the finished necklace.

Experiment

Get creative with how you use this hinge on bracelet links, earrings, or necklaces. This type of handmade hinge could apply to all sorts of projects, such as clasps for handmade books or hinges for handmade purses.

A simple hinge pattern to start you off

Using Color on Metals

COLOR IS INTEGRAL TO LIFE. Biologically, we connect to it at such a deep level that it affects our thoughts, our moods, and our every decision. Naturally, we long to apply color to metal, and some metals react to it more than others. We could write volumes on the subject of color on metal (some already have!), but instead, in this next unit, we explore just a few ways to achieve color on copper. It'll get you started on your metalsmithing path.

UNIT

7

Red floral form by Kathryn Osgood

Home Ammonia Patinas

Materials & Tools

- straw
- ammonia
- table salt
- plastic containers with lids
- copper pieces, clean and finished
- other materials such as sawdust or wood shavings

"Creativity is allowing yourself to make mistakes. Art is knowing which ones to keep."

—Scott Adams, creator of *Dilbert* cartoon

Copper is a very reactive metal, and when paired with household ammonia, it can result in a range of blues and greens traditionally called *verdigris*. With patinas that involve materials such as sawdust or straw, the material itself creates a pattern where it makes contact with the metal. With ammonia fume patinas, the fume reacts with salt and copper. These patinas are fragile and work best in grooves or protected areas of jewelry.

Clockwise from top right: copper and ammonia left in sawdust; ammonia fume patina on copper; copper, ammonia, and salt left in straw

Instructions

1. Drench the straw in a plastic tub by stirring in 1 to 2 tablespoons (15 to 30 ml) of ammonia. Also try adding a generous sprinkle of salt. Close the lid tightly and shake gently.

2. Prepare three pieces of copper with which to experiment.

3. Bury the copper pieces in the ammonia-coated straw.

4. Let the container with the straw and copper pieces sit for twenty-four hours.

5. Take one copper piece out at twenty-four hours, another at thirty-two, and a third at forty-eight. The true color will show up as they dry.

6. Repeat the process with other materials such as sawdust, burlap, rice, tobacco, or kitty litter.

Tip

Coat the patina-covered copper with a clear spray varnish. This process will change its appearance; it will no longer be vibrant.

Experiment

For a bluer patina, try an ammonia fume patina. Sprinkle salt on clean, barely damp, copper and suspend it over ammonia, close but not touching, in a airtight container for twenty-four hours or more. It will become more vibrant as it dries.

Ammonia fumes react with salt on copper and create a lovely speckled-blue patina.

Colored Pencil on Metal

- copper
- pickle
- gesso, white or black
- colored pencils, such as Prismacolor
- paintbrush

"There are only three colors, ten digits, and seven notes; it's what we do with them that's important."

—Jim Rohn, business philosopher

In this lab, we color metal using artist-quality colored pencil and a primer called gesso. Used in fine arts, this primer has a chalky "tooth" to it that allows paint and pigments to grip the surface. Gesso is available in traditional white, black, and now clear at any art supply store.

A brooch featuring colored pencil over copper by Katherine Osgood

Instructions

1. Etch your copper slightly. This gives it a tooth to grab the gesso and pencil. Leaving it in strong pickle overnight (or even a couple of days) might do the trick, or for a deeper etch, use ferric chloride. See Unit 2 for details about etching.

2. Brush gesso onto the metal and allow it to dry thoroughly.

3. Color your design onto your metal.

Experiment

Try using metal shapes or themes that lend themselves to color, such as fish or feathers. Also, experiment with etched textures under the gesso.

Tip

You can blend Prismacolor or other high-quality colored pencils with your fingers.

Using colored pencils on copper can produce interesting patterns in vibrant colors.

Peanut Oil Patina

- peanut oil
- copper, cleaned and finished
- water
- quench bowl
- paintbrush
- torch

"Patience is the companion of wisdom."

—Saint Augustine

Patinas can often include household solutions. Try this simple patina for lustrous, subtle color on copper. Much like seasoning a wok, the peanut oil is smoked onto the metal.

Instructions

1. Brush onto copper a thin layer of peanut oil.

2. Wipe off any dripping oil.

3. Slowly heat the oil with a gentle flame until you begin to see smoke. Turn off the torch and allow the glowing color to creep into the design. Quench in water before it gets too dark.

Darker streaks show up where the oil was brushed on.

Experiment

This patina pairs beautifully with three-dimensional forms because the streaking accents any curves. Try this lab with your results from Lab 18. Or how would fold-formed jewelry look with this patina?

Tip

If you go too far and the metal gets too hot and turns dark, burn it all off, pickle the metal, and start again.

A finished piece of jewelry using peanut oil patina

Contrasting finishes

- copper
- liver-of-sulfur patina
- table salt
- ammonia patina
- wet/dry sandpaper
- punch
- paintbrushes
- sanding pads, such as 3M
- burnisher, optional

Doubling up on some of these surface-design techniques is a great way to add interest and complexity to jewelry. Don't feel limited to one treatment, but rather layer different textures and patinas on the same piece. The more you play with patinas and surfaces, the more ideas you'll hold in your design arsenal and the more unique your pieces will become.

Instructions

1. Add depressions or raised areas to the copper using your punch. These areas are intended to capture and hold patina.
2. Apply liver-of-sulfur to areas of metal you want to darken.
3. Dampen an area slightly and sprinkle it with salt. Suspend the piece over ammonia to get a fume patina.
4. Sand off the ammonia patina from unwanted areas.

"One must have time to look, the patience to hear what the material has to say . . . and then an openness to let it come to you."

—Barbara McClintock, scientist and Nobel Prize winner

Experiment

Try a steel or agate burnisher. Also, burnish on certain edges only to get a high polish that reflects light.

Tip

When making a piece of jewelry with contrasting finishes, carefully plan your process. Patinas should be done last. You might even mask out or resist patinas with Vaseline or wax.

Consider how combining patinas can create a striking piece like this pouch pendant.

Flame Patina on Copper

- copper
- water
- quench bowl
- insulated tweezers
- solder brick, optional
- torch

"I try to apply colors like words that shape poems, like notes that shape music."

—Joan Miró, artist

This lab is just as simple as it sounds: Putting flame on copper. It's a mesmerizing patina to create, and though it is fragile, it can sometimes be captured under spray sealants. As with other ephemeral patinas, use this in areas on your jewelry slightly protected from wear such as indentions or cavities.

Copper cuff bracelets turn out stunningly when given a flame patina.

Instructions

1. Hold your copper in place using tweezers (or you can just lay it down on a solder brick) and gently warm it with a soft torch flame.

2. Move the torch around at ten-second intervals, until a rainbow begins to travel across the metal's surface.

3. Quench the copper in water when you achieve your desired look. The color will come back as the piece dries.

Experiment

Try this over a liver-of-sulfur patina. Or slowly heat up the copper on a cold stove burner or in a toaster oven.

Tip

Slow-slow-slow and even is the name of the game. Patience results in more vibrant color. When you finish torching, flip over the piece; sometimes the best color is actually on the underside where less oxygen gets to the metal.

Examples of the range of color available through flame on copper

Torch-Fired Enamel

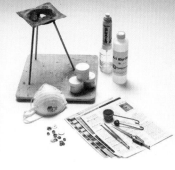

In this lab, we learn how easy and gratifying it is to fire glass enamel onto copper using a torch. Either an air/gas torch or a handheld propane bottle torch from a hardware store will work. An air/gas torch gives you greater control and freedom of movement. Use magazine pages as trays when sifting enamel. Use caution and always wear a mask—enamel is powdered glass.

- copper
- pickle
- old magazine pages
- dust mask
- gloves
- glass enamel powders
- holding agent, such as Klyr fire or hairspray
- punch
- drill, optional
- drill bits, optional
- dapping set
- aerosol spray bottle or paintbrush
- insulated tweezers
- enamel sifters
- soldering tripod or screen suspended over two firebricks
- torch

Firing enamel is easy and gratifying. These blossoms were colored by torch firing on enamel.

Instructions

1. Punch or drill out holes in copper discs, large enough for 20-gauge wire to go through easily.

2. Make half domes in different sizes out of your drilled discs using a dapping set. Make them irregular so they look more like flowers, or try snipping the edges into fringe.

3. Pickle the copper-dome shapes thoroughly.

4. Prepare a workstation while your pieces are pickling. Ready one magazine page per color you plan to sift to act as trays.

5. Put on a dust mask and gloves. Get out two or three colors to work with, and pour a few tablespoons into a sifter.

6. Remove the copper from the pickle, rinse, and dry.

7. Spray the inside of your copper piece with your holding agent. Use tweezers or a wire holder to hold your pieces.

Spray the piece or pieces with a holding agent.

Torch-fired enamel on copper components

Experiment

Enamel doesn't like direct torch heat from above. It draws up, pulls away, and often falls off the metal. However, here's another option: Dredge the hot metal through enamel powder to cause it to stick. If you choose to experiment this way, be careful and use insulated cross-locking tweezers and gloves. Up for something else? Try fusing on little beads or glass threads available from enamel suppliers.

8. Keep on your protective gear. Sift the enamel onto the damp copper piece.

9. Allow this to dry for three or four minutes.

10. Set down the piece on your tripod or firing area. Light the torch and begin heating from *underneath*. Heat the enamel until it glistens as if wet. Continue until it looks soft, dull orange, and wet like candy. Remove the heat and allow it to slowly cool. The color will appear as it cools.

Sift enamel onto the piece.

Set the piece on the firing area.

Tip

Many transparent enamels become more vibrant with overfiring. This means heating a bit longer than is necessary to flow enamel.

findings

8

JEWELRY PIECES NEED CONNEC-TIVE MECHANISMS to make them wearable. These—the clasps, ear wires, and chains—are usually called findings. Certainly many sturdy, professionally made options are available commercially. However, these can often seem sterile and uninteresting. Handmade findings, on the other hand, enhance the nature of your work and make it stand out in a crowd. In learning to incorporate these handmade elements, you can develop other ideas for connections and mechanisms. In fact, it can become quite an obsession thinking up new and ingenious ways to suspend or attach adornment to the human body.

Above: *Close detail of clasp*

UNIT

Hand-forged chain by Marion Sak

- half-round wire
- solder
- flux
- pickle
- round wire in various gauges, optional
- square wire in large gauges, optional
- wire-working pliers such as round-nose
- mandrels or straight punches
- flush-cutting pliers
- jeweler's saw
- third hand
- tweezers
- soldering surface
- torch
- round pliers

Making your own chain can produce a necklace or bracelet bursting with character and personality. No need to limit yourself to chains made of jump rings. Try forging out wire for more interesting variations.

Chain made of large, soldered, stretched jump rings and charm links

Instructions

Wrapping wire around a mandrel to create a jump ring

Sawing through jump rings

Stretch round links into ovals with pliers.

1. Make a coil of half-round wire around a large mandrel. Slide coil off.

2. Cut these into rings with flush cutters, or for a better, smoother seam, saw them.

3. Solder shut half of the rings. For example, if you made eight rings, solder four.

4. Use a third hand and tweezers to join the unsoldered coils to the already soldered ones. Add flux and a pallion of solder to the seams, and solder all of them closed.

5. Pickle clean and rinse.

6. Stretch out each of the links into long ovals using round pliers.

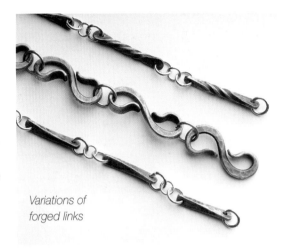

Variations of forged links

Experiment

Forging or drilling and then joining with jump rings can create interesting links for chains. Or try flattening out little segments of square wire with a hammer or annealing square segments of wire and twisting them with pliers.

Tip

Saw jump rings from a coil. Make a coil with wire and thread it onto a saw blade in a frame. Then you can hold the coil and saw your way from the inside of the coil out. Remember, always twist jump rings to open. Never spread them apart.

- metal
- pendant
- flux
- solder
- scribe
- saw
- needle files
- torch
- solder surface

"When you make the finding yourself—even if you're the last person on Earth to see the light—you'll never forget it."

—Carl Sagan, astronomer

Making your own parts usually results in more unique work. And the more you do yourself, the less tied your jewelry making is to what's available commercially. Bails connect a pendant to its chain. They can be as unique and individual as people.

A pendant with a large textured bail sawn from a sheet

Instructions

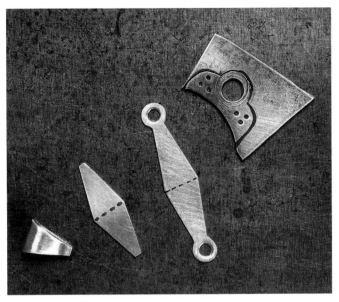

From right to left: A larger, fancy-shaped bail partially sawn from sheet; a triangular bail to be folded and riveted to a pendant; a triangular bail before folding; and a small folded triangular bail ready for soldering.

1. Scribe a diamond shape onto your metal that you can later fold to make a double *V*.
2. Cut out the shape.
3. Fold it over—gently—at the middle or widest part, leaving a soft opening for a chain.
4. Solder the bail, at its tip, to your pendant. Or leave two round areas that you can drill and rivet to your pendant.

Experiment

Tubing can make interesting bails, like those shown in the image. When soldering together the parts, use round needle files to file contours for a tighter fit.

Various bails constructed from silver tubing

Tip

If your pendant, when laid on its back, sits taller than the bail, lift the bail by stacking metal pieces or pennies under it. (Be sure to use old pennies so that they're truly copper.) Or use a third hand to align the pieces.

43 Toggles

- wire
- flux
- solder
- pickle
- torch
- pliers

"The image is more than an idea. It is a vortex or cluster of fused ideas and is endowed with energy."

—Ezra Pound, poet

Toggles, jewelry-closing or -clasping mechanisms that typically consist of a ring and a bar, can serve dual functions. They make great focal points for necklaces and bracelets and also serve as the clasp.

A bracelet made of beads and a fused silver toggle

Instructions

1. Collect some scrap and wire to fuse together.
2. Arrange the wire and scrap loosely in a round shape the size of toggle you want.
3. Flux everything generously.
4. Heat the wire gently with a torch until the metal collapses and melts together.
5. Repeat the process with a bar shape. Make it wider than the opening of the toggle.
6. Pickle until clean. Polish as needed.

Various toggles made from fused silver pieces

Experiment

Keep an eye out for found objects such as buttons that you can turn into toggles. Or saw toggles out of large pieces of textured metal. Refer back to some of the labs that involve etching to etch a large toggle centerpiece. Or roll mill texture onto a piece that might become a toggle.

Found objects to make into toggles and a bar made from thick copper ground wire from the hardware store

Tip

Copper doesn't like to fuse and has a very high melting point. So if you want to make a toggle out of cooper, add a bit of solder to connect your pieces. Also, using a bit of steel wool in tweezers, paint some old, blue-colored pickle on your solder spots. The steel reacts with the old pickle and copper-plates the solder.

Hooks and Ear Wires

- wire, 20-gauge
- pickle
- wet/dry sandpaper
- torch
- flush-cutting pliers
- hammer
- metal block

"A positive attitude causes a chain reaction of positive thoughts, events, and outcomes. It is a catalyst and it sparks extraordinary results."

—Wade Boggs,
baseball player

Hooks and ear wires are integral to the wearing of an earring or chain. But they can also be integral to its visual beauty and overall design. To get you started, this lab introduces you to simple French ear wires and forged hooks. There are many specialty pliers on the market for making precision ear wires and hooks, some of which can be pricey. For now, use round nose pliers. Metal punches and dowels can also make excellent mandrels for forming ear wires and clasps.

Multiple examples of ear wire and hook shapes

Instructions

1. Cut off 2½ to 3 inches (6.4 to 7.6 cm) of wire.

2. Ball the end with a torch. Pickle and rinse.

3. Curl up the ball using pliers to make a tight curl. This will hold the earring.

4. Bend the long leg around, again with pliers, to make the hook that will go through the ear.

5. Hammer the ear wire gently on a metal block to work-harden it. Hammer more in certain areas to spread out the metal.

Tip
Make hooks in much the same way. Use more substantial wire and hammer them to work harden.

Experiment
Try bending wires using many different methods. Wooden dowels or transfer punches make great forming tools. Clamp the punch in a vise and slightly hammer on the ear wires.

Use large round pliers to make ear wires.

Hammering an ear wire

Hammering on the end of the wire forges a paddle to make a hook

Alternative Methods and Materials

WE ARE FORTUNATE TO LIVE IN A TIME when anything goes in the art jewelry world. We can use bottle caps and other found objects, even dirt and living things. As humans continue to redefine and explore what it means to live here, in this time, jewelry has come to reflect that experience in the same fashion as have other art forms. In this final unit, we scratch the surface of the vast well of alternative materials available to jewelry makers.

UNIT 9

Bottle cap brooches by Betty McKim

Faux Concrete

- two-part epoxy putty
- plastic gloves
- bezel
- objects to trap
- razor blade

*"Just as we have two eyes
and two feet, duality is part
of life."*

—Carlos Santana, musician

There are many types of epoxy putty on the market. Some are steel-reinforced, which comes in handy if you need strength. Two-part putty often looks like concrete when cured, and can be used to trap found objects into bezels. It's a convenient, easy way to obtain a concrete or grout look with no measuring and minimal mixing.

A silver bezel with ammonite trapped in putty

Instructions

Slice off a piece of the two-part putty with a razor blade.

1. Slice off a small chunk of the two-part putty with the razor blade.
2. Knead the putty until it becomes a solid color. Follow package directions for correct mixing.
3. Push a small bit of putty into your bezel.
4. Push your object down into the putty while the putty's still soft.
5. Allow the piece to cure or set overnight (or according to package directions).

Tip
Use rubber-tipped clay working tools to smooth over putty.

Experiment
Try pushing the putty into a **push mold**. The putty can get sticky, so wait until it begins to cure and also use a releasing agent (available in hobby shops near the mold-making and -casting section).

Set all kinds of objects, like those shown here, into a bezel using two-part putty.

Materials & Tools

- color plastic,
  ⅛-inch (3 mm) thick
- saw blade wax
- round burrs
- heart burrs
- wet/dry sandpaper
- jeweler's saw
- 3/0 saw blades
- Dremel or flexshaft
- drill bits
- file

"The purpose of art is washing the dust of daily life off our souls."

—Pablo Picasso, artist

Plastic can be fun to work with. In this lab, we saw and burr-colored Plexiglas to make earrings and jewelry components.

Earrings made from blue Plexiglas

Instructions

1. Determine a shape for your earrings.

2. Lubricate your saw blade with a saw-and-burr wax, and then cut out your shape (see Lab 18 for directions on how to saw Plexiglas).

3. Make random partial cuts into the plastic using drill bits and burrs. These will slightly glow when light hits them.

4. Drill holes for ear wires.

5. File and sand edges.

6. Attach ear wires. These may need wider loops, depending on the thickness of the Plexiglas.

Tip

Use care when burring plastic. Burrs can take off when run too fast. You only need a partial indention to pick up the light, so go slowly.

Experiment

Before you work on your plastic, play around on a scrap sheet to see how different burrs leave different marks. You also might try sanding the Plexiglas to get a foggy look or filing it to make marks. Plastic can also be warmed with a heat gun or oven and bent over forms. Try warming the earrings and twisting them with pliers. It takes a minute or so for the plastic to cool and freeze in place. Be sure to ventilate!

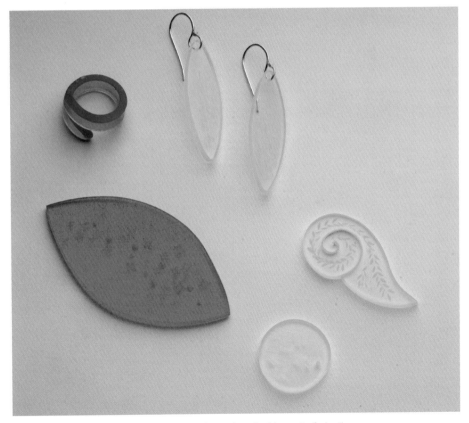

Make all kinds of jewelry, in almost any shape imaginable, out of plastic.

47 Plasti Dip

- Plasti Dip, one can
- wire in a variety of thicknesses
- newspaper
- findings
- wire-working pliers

"Go for it now. The future is promised to no one."

—Wayne Dyer, motivational speaker

Experiment with Plasti Dip, a commercial plastic material used to coat tool handles, available at your hardware store. This is a great means to take advantage of three-dimensional wire forms. The plastic unifies elements and plays up their sculptural nature.

Jewelry pieces made using Plasti Dip

Instructions

Note: Work in a place with ventilation or outside. Plasti Dip has a fume.

1. Set up a drying area with something from which to hang the pieces and lay down newspaper to protect underlying surfaces.

2. Create shapes out of wire to coat.

3. Using a hook and gloves, dip the wire shapes into the Plasti Dip, allowing excess plastic to drip off.

4. Hang up to dry and let it dry completely before moving to step 5.

5. Connect to jewelry findings such as ear wires, or hang on a chain.

Dipping metal into Plasti Dip

Experiment

Try combining wire and other objects or combining wire with polymer clay elements and then dipping them.

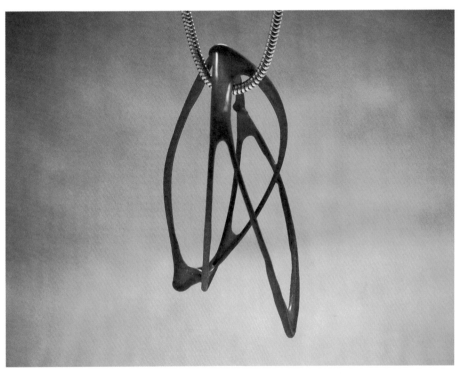

Pendant made of iron wire dipped in Plasti Dip

Tip

Plasti Dip usually comes in primary colors (red, yellow, and blue), though you can order it in custom colors, too!

Trapping felt and fabric

- metal
- felt or fabric
- wet/dry sandpaper
- black plate
- riveting materials
- jeweler's saw
- file
- drill
- drill bits
- scissors
- hammer
- metal block

Humans are tactile beings. We love to touch and feel. Jewelry, by its nature, requires contact with the hands, so why not add fiber and fabric to the equation?

A felt-and-silver ring by Sarah Tector

Instructions

1. Determine an open design that allows the felt or fabric to show.

2. Saw out design from your metal, and then file, sand, and finish the edges.

3. Drill holes to match your rivet material in the top sheet only.

4. Align the top and back sheet and drill one hole all the way through.

5. Add the felt or fabric in between. You may need to snip a hole through your fabric. Trim the fabric slightly smaller than your top sheet.

6. Set your first rivet through all layers. (See Labs 19 and 20 for detailed instructions on riveting.)

7. Repeat until all rivets are set.

Tip

Like with other found materials, any connection that does not require heat will works for felt or fabric.

Experiment

For a different or unique look, try fabric with a rich, tactile quality such as velvet or shag.

Felt trapped in metal with rivets

MOSS in Jewelry

- bezel
- moss, natural or artificial
- matt knife
- tweezers
- spray bottle

"Every moment and every event of every man's life on earth plants something in his soul."

—Thomas Merton, writer

Moss conjures images of moist, quiet forests, of fairies and princesses with spells cast upon them. It works really well in jewelry, and it grows in many places, if tended and kept moist. Purchase dried or imitation moss in most hobby stores. While you're there, explore the floral section, too. It can yield a plethora of materials and ideas.

In this pendant, dried moss is trapped between mica sheets.

Instructions

1. Construct a pendant or ring with a bezel deep enough for your moss and some dirt.

2. Take a walk. Find moss to spoon up and carry home. Get a little of its home dirt with it. Or head to the hobby store for artificial moss.

3. Using a matt knife and tweezers, cut out a piece of moss the size of your bezel.

4. Insert the moss into your bezel with a little of its dirt. Spritz with water.

5. Keep your moss alive by placing it under a glass jar with a little moisture, near a window with ambient—not direct—sunlight.

Tip

Keep moss moist. Think about the environments in which it typically lives. If you can't keep it moist, try imitation or dried moss.

Experiment

Think about ways to trap moss in tiny terrariums made of miniature bottles.

A finished moss ring

Using Sausage Casings

- wire
- gloves
- sausage casing
- bucket of water
- scissors
- tweezers, optional
- pliers

"Grant me some wild expressions, Heavens, or I shall burst."

—George Farquhar, dramatist

The first material man had at his disposal came from animals. Long ago, humans realized that animal membrane stretched and dried taut, allowed light to pass through, and accepted inks and dyes. So it's not that strange to think of sausage casing as a material for jewelry. In fact, sausage casing is great because its sticks to other things and itself without glue. When it dries, it becomes a translucent, paperlike tissue, and pulls taut over a frame. And, it comes cleaned and ready for making sausage, frozen, or packed in salt.

Vessel pendants and a ring of iron wire and sausage casing

Instructions

1. Prepare some wire forms to cover, much like papier mâché armatures.

2. Put on your gloves. Take the casings out of the package and cut off a few small pieces.

3. Soak a small amount of casing in warm water for an hour or so. Find the end of one, pry it open with three fingers, and snip the edge. Tear open the casing at the snip with both hands to spread it out.

Split casing, spread out, can be used like papier mâché.

4. Allow the casing to dry for just a few minutes, until it no longer glistens. It becomes a tackier consistency at this stage and sticks better.

5. Spread out the casing with your fingers and cover the wire forms. Fold or wrap bits around the wire and let it stick to itself. Use tweezers if you need to. The casing shrinks quite a bit as it dries, so your piece will look very different dry than wet. For durability, apply two coats of casing.

Tip

Once you have it the way you like, allow it to dry naturally. Using a hairdryer or another heat source might be too intense and may cause the casing to crack and split. Coat the whole piece with clear sprays and acrylic varnishes to preserve the look. If you don't spray iron wire, it will eventually rust, which adds an interesting look but can split through the casing with time.

Experiment

Flow dyes or inks onto the damp casing with a dropper or brushes. Once the casing dries, it becomes paperlike; stamp it, write on it, sew through it, you name it! The casing will be unwieldy at first, so don't make huge open areas to cover. Once you get the hang of using it, you'll be better able to determine which designs to work with.

Sausage casing dries taut over armatures and easily accepts ink and paint.

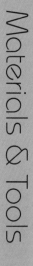

- silver
- jewelry components
- embroidery floss
- epoxy or glue
- drill
- bits
- needle
- scissors

"But even if I'm left high and dry at the end of this wild journey, just taking it is a great feeling."

—Olivia Wilde, actress

Combining materials can be a wonderful way to solve construction problems or just to add a twist to your design. Introducing threads and fibers to metal brings a new tactile quality to your work that can intrigue and draw in the viewer. Try this lab in which we drill holes to allow sewing on metal.

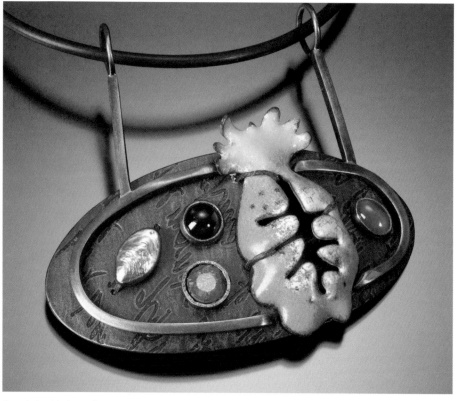

Seeds by Kathryn Osgood. Photo by Robert Diamante

Instructions

1. Cut a circle of silver.
2. Determine a design to drill onto your disc.
3. Dap it into a dome shape.
4. Drill holes for the stitches and for a jump ring from which to hang your pendant.
5. Choose a color and thread your needle.
6. Stitch your design onto your charm.

Experiment

Try stitching bracelet links together with fiber, or using stitches as cold connections. Also, try using different types and thicknesses of threads or fibers such as hemp, embroidery floss, yarn, or even recycled silk.

Tip

Adding a tiny dot of super glue or epoxy to your knot on the back prevents it from coming apart.

A silver pendant stitched with red embroidery floss

Vegan Ivory

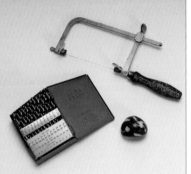

Tagua nut comes from a palm in South America, but you can find it at woodworking or carving suppliers. It can be sawn, carved with rotary tools, wood or linoleum carving tools, and dyed. This nut may look like conventional ivory but it's all vegetable, and increased interest in it has stimulated small businesses in many countries and preserved forests there. It is a great alternative for those who wish to use bone-colored material but prefer not to use animal products.

- tagua nut
- safety glasses
- gloves
- craft acrylic paint
- jeweler's saw
- skip-a-tooth saw blades
- coarse files or wood rasps
- carving tools
- rotary drill such as a Dremel and bits
- small vise

"Where the material ends, art begins."

—Étienne Hajdú, sculptor

A bird pendant made from tagua nut

Instructions

Jewelry makers who want to use ivory-colored material but prefer not to use animal products find tagua nut a suitable alternative.

1. Saw off a slice of a tagua nut. They often have cavities in the center that you will work around.
2. Remove the outer brown husk using a coarse file or rasp.
3. Begin to shape the slice with your saw.
4. Refine the edges with the coarse file.
5. Incise details using carving tools or your Dremel.
6. Apply craft paints so they embed into the carved areas. Wipe the surface to bring out the patterns.

Tip

When using drill bits or burrs, allow the nut and the bit to cool periodically. If you go too fast, you can melt and burn the nut.

Experiment

A small Japanese-style woodcutting saw from the hardware store makes a great tool for working this material. But be careful. It's easy to slip and cut yourself when using cutting tools to carve the tagua nut.

Use files to shape and refine your vegan ivory.

Glossary

Annealing: Softening metal through heating

Bench pin: A wooden, *V*-shaped form for sawing with a jeweler's saw

Bezel: A loop of metal pushed over to hold in a stone or object

Brown & Sharpe gauge: A round metal gauge with a series of slots to measure the thicknesses of sheet metals

Calipers: A tool used to measure the distance or thickness between two points

Center punch: A pointed metal punch for making small divots in metal

Dapping: Doming a disc

Dapping block: A block with multiple depressions or cavities for doming metal discs

Disc cutter: A metal device with punches for chopping out metal discs

Dividers: Pointed metal tools held together at the apex with a wing nut that allow you to measure even increments and widths

Findings: Small connective parts that make jewelry wearable such as jump rings, clasps, and ear wires

Firescale: The usually black build up of oxidation on metal. It can flake off or be removed by sanding or an acid bath called pickle.

Flux: A paste or liquid that protects a solder joint from oxygen and oxidation during soldering, thereby allowing the solder to flow

Jump ring: A round ring that joins together two pieces, like a charm to a chain. It jumps the gap between components.

Klyr fire: A clear liquid holding agent to hold the sugary dry enamel on the metal until it melts

Liver of sulfur: A sulfurated potash that reacts with metal and is used to darken and patina copper and silver

Mandrel: Any tool that material is shaped against

Millimeter gauge: A small, brass sliding gauge used for measuring diameters and lengths often in both millimeters and inches. They are also available in digital forms.

Pallion: A small chip or pellet of solder

Patina: A color on metal produced by oxidation or by chemical reaction

Peen: The end of a hammer such as a ball peen or cross peen. This can also refer to the mark left by a hammer strike.

Pickle: A mild acid used for cleaning firescale off of metal

Pin vise: A small hand vise shaped like a pen that can hold small tools such as drill bits

Precision square: An *L*-shaped tool used to make precise 90-degree angles.

Punch: A steel rod with a shaped tip at one end and a blunt butt end at the other, usually struck by a hammer to sculpt metal. There are many types of punches: transfer or conical-pointed round punches, center, dapping and chasing punches.

Push mold: Plastic half-molds available at hobby shops and polymer clay suppliers into which you can push clay. They come in endless shapes and sizes.

Quenching: Quickly cooling metal in water or sometimes oil

Scribe: A pointed tool used to scribe or mark lines onto metal

Skip-a-tooth blade: A saw blade missing every other blade, good for sawing through wood or Plexiglas

Sodium bisulfate: A dry, granular acid for use as pickle, for cleaning metal

Solder: A fusible metal alloy for joining metals, from the Latin *solidare*, meaning "to make solid"

Sparex: A brand of dry, granular acid for use as pickle, for cleaning metal.

Split mandrel: A piece of metal with a slit in it into which you can insert a strip of sandpaper for finishing metal with a rotary device such as a Dremel or a flexible shaft machine

Third hand: A heavy base with a set of swiveling tweezers attached for gripping objects and holding them in place during soldering or gluing

Toggle: A jewelry-closing or -clasping mechanism that typically consists of a ring and a bar. The bar slides through the ring and locks on the other side.

Work hardening: To make metal stiffer by hammering or working, which compresses the molecules tightly together, limiting mobility. Annealing reverses the process.

Helpful Charts—Relative Sizes Chart

B&S Gauge	mm	Inches Thousandths	Inches Fractions	Drill-bit size	B&S Gauge	mm	Inches Thousandths	Inches Fractions	Drill-bit size
0	8.5	.325	$21/64$		16	1.29	.050		54
1	7.35	.289	$9/32$		17	1.15	.045	$3/64$	55
2	6.54	.258	$1/4$		18	1.02	.040		56
3	5.83	.229	$7/32$	1	19	.912	.036		60
4	5.19	.204	$13/64$	6	20	.813	.032	$1/32$	65
5	4.62	.182	$3/16$	15	21	.724	.029		67
6	4.11	.162	$5/32$	20	22	.643	.025		70
7	3.67	.144	$9/64$	27	23	.574	.023		71
8	3.26	.129	$1/8$	30	24	.511	.020		74
10	2.59	.102		38	25	.455	.018		75
11	2.30	.090	$3/32$	43	26	.404	.016	$1/64$	77
12	2.05	.080	$5/64$	46	27	.361	.014		78
13	1.83	.072		50	28	.330	.013		79
14	1.63	.064	$1/16$	51	29	.278	.011		80
15	1.45	.057		52	30	.254	.010		

Determining Ring Blank Lengths

Sizes	Length-mm (paper strip)	Metal Thicknesses in B&S Gauges						
		12	14	16	18	20	22	24
1	39.0	45.5	44.2	43.0	42.1	41.5	40.9	40.5
1¼	39.6	46.2	44.6	43.6	42.7	42.1	41.5	41.1
1½	40.2	46.9	45.2	44.3	43.3	42.7	42.1	41.8
1¾	40.8	47.7	45.8	44.9	44.0	43.3	42.7	42.4
2	41.5	48.0	46.5	45.5	44.6	44.0	43.3	43.0
2¼	42.1	48.7	47.1	46.2	45.2	44.6	44.0	43.6
2½	42.7	49.3	47.7	46.8	45.8	45.2	44.6	44.3
2¾	43.3	49.9	48.4	47.4	46.5	45.8	45.2	44.9
3	44.0	50.6	49.0	48.0	47.1	46.5	45.8	45.6
3¼	44.6	51.2	49.6	48.7	47.7	47.1	46.5	46.2
3½	45.2	51.8	50.2	49.3	48.4	47.7	47.1	46.8
3¾	45.9	52.4	50.9	49.9	49.0	48.4	47.7	47.4
4	46.5	53.1	51.5	50.6	49.6	49.0	48.3	48.0
4¼	47.1	53.7	52.1	51.2	50.2	49.6	49.0	48.7
4½	47.8	54.3	52.8	51.8	50.9	50.2	49.6	49.3
4¾	48.4	55.0	53.4	52.4	51.5	50.9	50.2	49.9
5	49.0	55.6	54.0	53.1	52.1	51.5	50.9	50.6
5¼	49.6	56.2	54.6	53.7	52.8	52.1	51.5	51.2
5½	50.3	56.8	55.3	54.3	53.4	52.7	52.1	51.8
5¾	50.9	57.5	55.9	55.0	54.0	53.4	52.8	52.4
6	51.5	58.1	56.5	55.6	54.6	54.0	53.4	53.1
6¼	52.2	58.7	57.1	56.2	55.3	54.6	54.0	53.7
6½	52.8	59.3	57.8	56.8	55.9	55.3	54.6	54.3
6¾	53.4	60.0	58.4	57.5	56.5	55.9	55.3	55.0
7	54.0	60.6	59.0	58.1	57.1	56.5	55.9	55.6
7¼	54.7	61.2	59.7	58.7	57.8	57.1	56.5	56.2
7½	55.3	61.9	60.3	59.3	58.4	57.8	57.1	56.8
7¾	55.9	62.5	60.9	60.0	59.0	58.4	57.8	57.5

Add 0.5 mm to these lengths if the band is wider/taller than 4 mm.

Sizes	Length-mm (paper strip)	Metal Thicknesses in B&S Gauges						
		12	14	16	18	20	22	24
8	56.6	63.1	61.5	60.6	59.7	59.0	58.4	58.1
8¼	57.2	63.7	62.2	61.2	60.3	59.7	59.0	58.7
8½	57.8	64.4	62.8	61.9	60.9	60.3	59.7	59.2
8¾	58.4	65.0	63.4	62.5	61.5	60.9	60.3	60.0
9	59.1	65.6	64.1	63.1	62.2	61.5	60.9	60.6
9¼	59.7	66.3	64.7	63.7	62.8	62.2	61.5	61.2
9½	60.3	66.9	65.3	64.4	63.4	62.8	62.2	61.9
9¾	60.9	67.5	65.9	65.0	64.1	63.4	62.8	62.5
10	61.6	68.1	66.6	65.6	64.7	64.1	63.4	63.1
10¼	62.2	68.8	67.2	66.3	65.3	64.7	64.1	63.7
10½	62.8	69.4	67.8	66.9	65.9	65.3	64.7	64.4
10¾	63.5	70.0	68.5	67.6	66.6	65.9	65.3	65.0
11	64.1	70.1	69.1	68.1	67.2	66.6	65.9	65.6
11¼	64.7	71.3	69.7	68.8	67.8	67.2	66.6	66.3
11½	65.3	71.9	70.3	69.4	68.5	67.8	67.2	66.9
11¾	66.0	72.5	71.0	70.0	69.1	68.5	67.8	67.5
12	66.6	73.2	71.6	70.7	69.7	69.1	68.5	68.1
12¼	67.2	73.8	72.2	71.3	70.3	69.7	69.1	68.8
12½	67.9	74.4	72.8	71.9	71.0	70.3	69.7	69.4
12 ¾	68.5	75.0	73.5	72.5	71.6	71.0	70.3	70.0
13	69.1	75.7	74.1	73.2	72.2	71.6	71.0	70.7

Add 0.5 mm to these lengths if the band is wider/taller than 4 mm.

Resources

Edinburgh Etch

www.polymetaal.nl/beguin/mape/edinburgh_etch.htm

Enamels and Supplies

Thompson Enamel: www.thompsonenamel.com

Etching Mordants

Blick Art Materials: www.dickblick.com/categories/etchingchemicals

Graphic Chemical: www.graphicchemical.com

Rio Grande: www.riogrande.com

Etching Resists

Blick Art Materials: www.dickblick.com/categories/etchingchemicals/

Graphic Chemical: www.graphicchemical.com

Dip Micro: www.dipmicro.com/store/PNPB

Techniks: www.techniks.com

Miniature Nuts and Bolts

Micro-Mark: www.micromark.com

Reactive Metals Studio: www.reactivemetals.com

Scale Hardware: www.scalehardware.com/

RAW MATERIALS
Silver and Gold

Hauser & Miller Co.: www.hauserandmiller.com

Hoover & Strong: www.hooverandstrong.com

Rio Grande: www.riogrande.com

Copper and Other Metals

The Contenti Company: www.contenti.com

Metalliferous: www.metalliferous.com

Rio Grande: www.riogrande.com

T. B. Hagstoz & Son: www.hagstoz.com

Sausage Casings

Try your local butcher first.

Ask the Meatman: www.askthemeatman.com/sausage_casings.htm

The Sausage Maker, Inc.: www.sausagemaker.com

Wells Pork and Beef: www.wellsporkandbeef.com

Specialty Tools

This includes pliers, sparex and other pickles, copper tongs, torches, solders, and fluxes.

The Contenti Company: www.contenti.com

Metalliferous: www.metalliferous.com

Otto Frei: www.ottofrei.com

Rio Grande: www.riogrande.com

Tagua Nut

And tools for working with it

Lee Valley Tools Ltd.: www.leevalley.com

The Woodturners Catalog: www.woodturnerscatalog.com

Two-Part Epoxy Putty

Check your local hardware stores.

Micro-Mark: www.micromark.com/

Sherri Haab Shop: www.sherrihaab-shop.com/resin-supplies.html

Places to Learn More

Arrowmont School of Arts and Crafts
www.arrowmont.org

Bear Canyon School of Art and Craft
www.bearcanyonschool.com

Haystack Mountain School of Crafts
www.haystack-mtn.org

John C. Campbell Folk School
www.folkschool.org

Metal Cyberspace
www.metalcyberspace.com

Penland School of Crafts
www.penland.org

Peters Valley Craft Center
www.petersvalley.org

The Ranch Center for Arts and Crafts
www.artattheranch.com

Photo by Robert Diamante

Bezel set enamel by Adrienne Grafton

Acknowledgments

I would like to express my sincere thanks and overwhelming gratitude to Mary Ellen Golden and John W. Golden for their unending encouragement and support over the years. I also wish to thank Linda Darty for taking a chance on me, and Bob Ebendorf for convincing her to do so! I extend my appreciation to Tim Lazure, as well as my grad school compadres without whom I could not have written this book, especially The Slot Machines. I'd like to extend a special thank you Adrienne Grafton, Kate Cathey, Kathryn Osgood, Betty McKim, Nick Mowers, Marion Sak, Sarah Tector, Gail Marcus, Gabriel Vohryzek Lombardi, and Sara Westermark for their lovely contributions to this book. And thanks to Beth Hammett for the use of her torch, and to Sherri Haab for turning me onto and supplying me with her great two-part putty. And thank you to my friends Traci Bunkers, LK Ludwig, and Bee Shay for their encouragement. And thank you to my agent, Neil Salkind.

Also deserving of my earnest thanks are Joshua Curry for sharing his great talent and being so generous with his patience, and Bethany Otten for her lovely hands! I wish to also thank Mary Ann Hall, Betsy Gammons, and Michele Wilson for for their guidance and hard work, along with all the folks at Quarry Books who had a hand in this publication. And a very deep, heartfelt thank you to my family, especially my parents, who held down the fort so I could go become something. Robert and Meredith deserve my deepest thanks for being my underpinnings. I could not have done this without Robert's careful nurturing and tending, and Meredith's lovely hands as well, and her resilient patience.

Finally, I wish to express my gratitude to my many students who were the guinea pigs. I am ever finely honed by my interactions with you who make it all worthwhile. Hammer on!

About the Author

Melissa Manley lives and works in southeastern North Carolina, a few miles from Wrightsville Beach. She received her bachelor of arts in studio arts from the University of North Carolina at Wilmington and earned her masters of fine arts in metal design at East Carolina University in 2006.

Melissa now teaches metals and jewelry making at Cape Fear Community College in Wilmington. For the past seven years, she has taught workshops around the country in many subjects, including collage, book altering, watercolor, and jewelry making. Her work has appeared in *Somerset Studio* magazine, *Crafting Personal Shrines* by Carol Owen, *The Art of Enameling* by Linda Darty, *Making Connections* by Susan Lenart Kazmer, and *500 Enameled Objects* by Lark books.

For more information about Melissa, visit www.melissamanleystudios.com/ or melissamanleystudios.blogspot.com/.